Juliann

THE
BONTEMPI COOKBOOK

By FEDORA BONTEMPI

PRENTICE-HALL, Inc., Englewood Cliffs, N. J.

To the TV viewers who turned us
on instead of off;

To the many sponsors who made our
TV program possible;

To my husband for his songs and for
his patience while oft competing
with the sound of mixers,
pots, and pans;

and

To my daughter for just her love.

Drawings by Janet Anderson

The Bontempi Cookbook, by Fedora Bontempi

© 1965 by Fedora Bontempi

All rights reserved, including the right to reproduce this book,
or any portions thereof, in any form except for the inclusion
of brief quotations in a review.

Library of Congress Catalog Card Number: 65-20233

Printed in the United States of America
T 07976

PRENTICE-HALL INTERNATIONAL, INC., *London*
PRENTICE-HALL OF AUSTRALIA, PTY., LTD., *Sydney*
PRENTICE-HALL OF CANADA, LTD., *Toronto*
PRENTICE-HALL OF INDIA (PRIVATE) LTD., *New Delhi*
PRENTICE-HALL OF JAPAN, INC., *Tokyo*

The intention of every other piece of prose may be discussed and even mistrusted; but the purpose of a cookery book is one and unmistakable. Its object can conceivably be no other than to increase the happiness of mankind.

Joseph Conrad

FOREWORD

My husband, Pino, and I are now in our sixteenth year on television, and we are told that this is a remarkable achievement. All I know is that it has been a great deal of fun cooking my way through those years—mainly because of the devotion of our viewers. This book is the answer to their devotion and to the oft-repeated wishes in their letters to us that the recipes we have brought to them via our programs be compiled in book form.

My one big problem was selecting the most popular recipes from the more than 8,000 dishes that I have prepared in full view of the television audience over this sixteen-year period. These included recipes of all lands and if this book has more than a proportionate share of Italian dishes, it is because these recipes were by far the most popular. We were able to gauge the popularity of a recipe through the mail requests. Some of these recipes brought in as many as 3,000 or 4,000 requests.

I have derived a great deal of pleasure in preparing this book, keeping in mind the many kind expressions of encouragement from our viewers. *The Bontempi Cookbook* is dedicated to them—for their warm and spontaneous approval of our efforts. My husband and I sincerely hope that the general public will also find it useful and helpful.

iii

I have tried to collect recipes that are not only exciting, but also practical and easy to prepare. They are all authentic.

It is our sincere wish that the homemaker or amateur chef will enjoy preparing these recipes and that they will bring a little more joy and happiness to the family dinner table.

Fedora Bontempi

CONTENTS

I   Appetizers   1

II   Soups   7

III   Eggs   15

IV   Fish   23

V   Poultry   39

VI   Meats: 57
          a) Beef   59
          b) Lamb   79
          c) Pork   89
          d) Veal   96

VII   Vegetables   113

VIII   Potatoes   135

IX   Rice   141

X   Pasta: 151
          a) Lasagna   153
          b) Macaroni   156
          c) Noodles   171
          d) Spaghetti   175

XI   Sauces   181

XII   Salads   191

XIII   Miscellaneous   199

XIV   Desserts: 207
     a) Cakes   209
     b) Cookies   219
     c) Fancy   222
     d) Pastries   226
     e) Pies   234

Glossary   240

Index   246

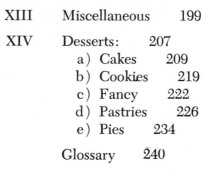

1
APPETIZERS

BAKED CLAMS, OREGANO

2 dozen cherrystone or littleneck clams on half
shell
¼ cup olive oil, approxi-
mately
2 cloves garlic, chopped
fine
pinch of black pepper

2 tablespoons chopped
parsley
1 cup bread crumbs
2 tablespoons grated
Parmesan cheese
1 teaspoon oregano
lemon wedges

*A delicious hot appetizer from sunny Naples. For more zest
a little red pepper may be added. These can be baked or
broiled—I prefer them broiled quickly, so as not to overcook
the clam.*

Arrange clams in a baking pan. Combine olive oil, garlic,
pepper, parsley, bread crumbs, cheese and oregano and mix
well together. Mixture should not be too dry or too moist. A
little clam juice may be added if too dry. Pile a little of this
mixture on each clam, covering clam completely. Broil under
moderate heat until crumb mixture browns lightly and crisps.
Watch carefully so as not to cook clams too much (they will
harden). Clams should be soft and juicy under browned crumb
mixture. Serve immediately with lemon wedges. *Serves 4.*

CHICKEN LIVER AND ANCHOVY CANAPÉ

8 to 10 chicken livers
1 tablespoon minced
   parsley
3 tablespoons butter
4 anchovy fillets, minced
dash of pepper

½ tablespoon flour
2 tablespoons chicken
   bouillon
1 tablespoon lemon juice
8 triangles of toast

Chop livers very fine and sauté with parsley in hot butter for about 5 or 6 minutes. Add anchovies, pepper and sprinkle with flour. Add bouillon, raise heat and, stirring constantly, cook for a minute or two longer. Remove from fire, stir in lemon juice. Spread on toast triangles and serve immediately. *Serves 4.*

BROILED SHRIMP, GOURMET

16 jumbo shrimp
½ cup cognac or sherry
thin slices prosciutto or
   bacon
sage leaves

lemon wedges
salt and pepper
4 skewers
bread crumbs

From the Adriatic comes this superb Scampi recipe.

Wash, rinse and drain shrimp. Remove shell, split along back, and devein. Place in shallow bowl, pour over cognac or sherry and set aside to marinate for about 1 hour, turning occasionally. Cut slices of prosciutto or bacon in pieces just large enough to wrap around each shrimp. Remove shrimp from marinade, dip in bread crumbs and wrap a piece of prosciutto or bacon around each shrimp. Run a skewer through prepared shrimp with sage leaf between shrimps. Place on boiler pan and broil under moderate heat, turning often and as prosciutto or bacon begins to crisp, sprinkle lightly with bread crumbs to form a fine crisp crust over shrimp. Season lightly with salt and pepper and remove skewers. Serve hot with lemon wedges. Figure on 4 shrimp per serving. *Serves 4.*

4

OVEN-FRIED CURRIED SHRIMP IN HOT DIP

2 lbs. shrimp, fresh or
    frozen
1 egg, beaten
1 tablespoon water
1 cup dry bread crumbs,
    toasted

2 teaspoons curry powder
½ teaspoon salt
dash pepper
¼ cup olive oil
* Hot Marmalade Soy Dip

Thaw frozen shrimp. Peel fresh shrimp. Remove sand veins and wash. Combine egg and water. Combine crumbs, curry powder, salt and pepper. Dip shrimp in egg and roll in crumbs. Arrange in one layer in a well-greased shallow baking pan. Drizzle olive oil over shrimp. Bake in a very hot 500° F. oven for 10 to 15 minutes, or until golden brown. Serve with Hot Marmalade Soy Dip. *Serves 4 to 6.*

* *Hot Marmalade Soy Dip:* Combine ⅓ cup orange marmalade, ¼ cup lemon juice, ¼ cup soy sauce, 1 clove garlic, finely chopped, and a dash of ginger; bring to the boiling point. Dissolve 1 teaspoon cornstarch in 1 tablespoon cold water. Add to hot sauce and cook until thickened, stirring constantly. Serve hot. *Makes approximately 1 cup of dip.*

2
SOUPS

BEAN AND MACARONI SOUP ALLA ROMANA

⅛ lb. salt pork
1 medium onion
1 clove garlic
1 stalk celery
2 tablespoons olive oil
½ 16-oz. can tomatoes, drained and crushed
1 teaspoon salt

½ teaspoon pepper
1 quart warm water
½ lb. ditali (or elbow macaroni)
1 can cannellini (white kidney beans)
grated Parmesan cheese

This is the thick and succulent "Pasta e Fagioli."

Chop the salt pork, onion, garlic and celery all together very fine. Brown well in olive oil in large saucepan. Add tomatoes, salt and pepper, warm water and bring to boil. Add macaroni and cook for about 8 to 10 minutes or until almost tender, then add can of beans without draining. Mix, cover and cook for another 5 minutes or until macaroni is tender. Serve sprinkled with grated cheese. *Serves 4 to 6.*

CHICKEN VEGETABLE SOUP WITH MEATBALLS

3 to 4 quarts chicken
   broth
3 carrots, thinly sliced
2 potatoes, diced very
   small
1½ cups fresh green peas

MEATBALLS

½ lb. ground beef
1 egg
½ tablespoon grated
   Parmesan cheese
salt and pepper to taste
bread crumbs

Prepare meatballs as follows: combine ingredients and blend well by hand, adding a small amount of bread crumbs if mixture is too thin, and then shape into very tiny meatballs, not much larger than a large green pea. Bring chicken broth to a boil, add vegetables and prepared meatballs; bring back quickly to a rolling boil, then reduce heat and let simmer gently, covered, for about 30 minutes until all ingredients are done. Serve hot with grated Parmesan cheese. Thin slivers of boiled chicken may also be added as well as rice or a fine pastina. *Serves 6.*

ROMAN EGG-DROP SOUP

1 quart chicken or beef
   broth
3 eggs
2 tablespoons semolina
   (Farina)

3 tablespoons grated
   Parmesan cheese
pinch of nutmeg
   (optional)
pinch of salt

This famous Roman soup "Stracciatella" is light and airy and yet has substance. To obtain this result the beaten egg mixture must be added to the boiling broth ever so slowly in a fine, thin stream while beating the broth constantly with a wire whisk—and continuing to beat until the egg is thoroughly cooked, light, and in tiny flakes.

Combine eggs, semolina, cheese, nutmeg and salt in a bowl with about ¼ cup of cold broth and beat well. Bring broth to boil, add egg mixture as directed above, and serve hot. *Serves 4.*

ONION AND EGG SOUP

¼ lb. butter (1 stick)	salt to taste
3 large onions, very thinly sliced	4 egg yolks
2 tablespoons flour	6 tablespoons grated Parmesan cheese
1½ quarts chicken or beef broth	thin slices of Italian or French bread, toasted

The Italians have their own version of onion soup—they add to it a thin stream of beaten egg yolks—a combination of the famous Roman "Stracciatella" and the French onion soup.

Melt butter in soup pan, add onion and sauté slowly until onion is soft and dark gold in color. Stir in flour and blend well. Add broth; salt to taste. Cover pan and simmer gently for about 30 minutes. Beat egg yolks lightly in mixing bowl and stir in cheese. Add slowly to soup, while whipping with a wire beater until egg is thoroughly cooked and in tiny frothy flakes. Serve with toasted bread and more grated cheese if desired. Serves *4 to 6.*

BEAN AND CABBAGE SOUP, FLORENTINE

2 tablespoons olive oil
1 onion, minced
1 small clove garlic,
    whole
2 slices prosciutto, cut up
½ head Savoy cabbage,
    cut up coarsely
2 small stalks celery,
    chopped
1 leek, minced
1 small ham bone
2 tablespoons tomato
    paste
thyme
2 cans cannellini (white
    kidney beans) or red
    kidney beans

1 quart water, broth or
    bouillon
salt and pepper
toasted slices Italian
    black bread (whole
    wheat)
grated Parmesan cheese

SOFFRITTO

2 tablespoons olive oil
1 teaspoon rosemary
pinch of thyme
2 cloves garlic, whole
    and crushed

Tuscans are soup and bean lovers. Here the Florentines combine their beloved beans with the rich, wrinkled Savoy cabbage and a blend of savory herbs into a delicious thick concoction that can almost be cut with a knife.

Brown the onion, 1 clove garlic and prosciutto in ¼ cup olive oil in a large soup pan. When nicely browned, add shredded cabbage, celery, leek, ham bone, tomato paste and a pinch of thyme. Mix well and sauté until vegetables are softened, stirring frequently. Meanwhile put one can of beans through a fine strainer or ricer, adding a quart of water or broth to make a thin purée. Add this purée to vegetables; salt and pepper to taste; mix well, cover and let simmer gently for about 1 hour. When minestrone is done, prepare the "soffritto" or herbed olive oil, which is all-important in this Florentine specialty. Pour ¼ cup olive oil into a small frying pan, add the rosemary, thyme and two cloves of garlic and sear or brown quickly over a high flame until garlic starts to color. Strain this aromatic oil into the soup. Add the remaining can of beans. Stir mine-

12

strone thoroughly and let boil gently for another 10 or 15 minutes, so that it absorbs this pungent flavoring. Remove ham bone. Serve in large, deep serving dish, soup tureen, or individual soup plates over a layer of toasted slices of Italian black bread (preferably day-old bread), with a sprinkling of grated cheese. This can be served hot or cold—it is delicious both ways. *Serves 4 to 6.*

3
EGGS

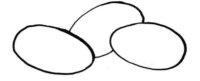

BAKED EGGS IN TOMATO CASES

4 large tomatoes   ½ cup bread crumbs
4 eggs

Cut a slice from the stem end of tomatoes, remove pulp to form a cavity, break and drop an egg into each tomato, sprinkle with salt and pepper and cover with bread crumbs. Place in shallow greased oven dish, bake for 20 minutes at 350° F. or until egg white is set. Serve hot. *Serves 4.*

BAKED EGGS WITH POTATOES AND CHEESE

4 medium-sized boiled   ½ teaspoon salt
    potatoes, sliced   ¼ teaspoon pepper
½ lb. mozzarella or Swiss   4 tablespoons grated
    cheese, sliced thin   Parmesan cheese
4 eggs   1 tablespoon butter

Arrange potatoes in a buttered shallow baking dish; arrange mozzarella slices over them and break eggs gently over mozzarella. Sprinkle with salt, pepper and grated cheese; dot with butter and bake in hot oven (400° F.) for 20 minutes or until eggs are set and cheese melted. Serve immediately! *Serves 2 to 4.*

EGG AND CHEESE PIE

4 eggs

4 tablespoons flour

1 cup milk

¼ lb. grated mozzarella
or Swiss cheese

2 tablespoons butter,
melted

salt and pepper

Beat eggs well, adding flour gradually. Continue beating and gradually add milk, mozzarella cheese, butter and salt and pepper to taste. Turn into buttered pie plate or pan and bake in hot 450° F. oven for about 30 minutes. The torte should swell and have a golden crusty top. Cut like pie and serve with meat, fish or fowl. *Serves 4.*

EGGS, PARMESAN STYLE

Butter a shallow baking dish, break 2 eggs into dish, sprinkle with a few slivers of ham or prosciutto; then sprinkle generously with grated Parmesan cheese. Bake in hot oven until eggs are set and cheese melted. Serve hot! *Serves 1.*

EGGS IN TOMATO SAUCE

Slightly brown a crushed whole clove of garlic in one or two tablespoons of hot olive oil in a skillet. Add half of 16-oz. can of tomatoes, breaking them up with a fork; season with salt and pepper and add a pinch of sugar. Simmer for 4 or 5 minutes; remove garlic. Gently break 4 eggs over tomatoes and cook until eggs have set. *Serves 2.*

FRIED CHEESE-STUFFED EGGS

4 hard-cooked eggs	pinch of nutmeg
½ lb. ricotta or cottage cheese	flour
	1 egg, lightly beaten
1 tablespoon grated Parmesan cheese	bread crumbs
	olive oil
salt and pepper	

If cottage cheese is used, be sure to pass it through a sieve.

Cut eggs in half and carefully remove yolks. Pass yolks through ricer or strainer and place in bowl, adding ricotta, grated Parmesan cheese, salt and pepper (to taste) and nutmeg. Mix thoroughly and fill cavity of each white egg with this egg mixture, heaping and spreading to edges, so that each half of egg white resembles a whole egg in shape. You will have 8 stuffed eggs. Roll each egg in flour very carefully, dip in beaten egg, roll in bread crumbs and fry in deep hot olive oil until golden brown on all sides. Serves hot. *Serves 2 to 4.*

QUICK MANICOTTI

FILLING

½ to 1 lb. ricotta cheese	salt and pepper to taste
¼ lb. mozzarella, finely diced or grated	pinch of sugar (optional)
	dash of nutmeg
1 or 2 tablespoons grated Parmesan cheese	milk

Mix all ingredients, blending well together, adding a little milk to make a smooth mixture.

CRÊPES

½ cup milk	⅛ teaspoon salt
scant ½ cup flour	1 tablespoon melted butter
4 eggs, slightly beaten	

Stir milk and flour together until smooth and, stirring constantly, add the eggs, salt and melted butter. Melt and heat a little butter, as needed, in a 6-inch frying pan. Pour four or five tablespoons of egg mixture into pan, tilting pan back and forth so it spreads evenly, and allow bottom to set; turn and let other side set. Slide from pan and set aside. When crêpes are all done place a small amount of filling in the center of each, fold one edge over and roll up. Arrange stuffed crêpes in a well-buttered baking dish, in one layer; dot generously with butter, sprinkle with grated Parmesan cheese and bake in a preheated 350° F. oven for about 15 to 20 minutes or until mozzarella cheese is melted. *Serves 4.*

Variations: diced prosciutto, ham or tiny pieces of cooked sausages may be added to filling. Crêpes may also be baked covered with tomato sauce and sprinkled with grated Parmesan or Romano cheese.

BAKED MOZZARELLA OMELETTE

2 tablespoons flour
2 tablespoons milk
4 eggs
⅛ teaspoon salt
3 tablespoons olive oil
½ lb. mozzarella cheese,
    sliced very thin

freshly ground pepper
chopped parsley
Parmesan cheese
    (optional)

Mix flour and milk, add eggs and salt; beat. Using an 8- or 9-inch oven-proof skillet, heat olive oil until very hot; pour egg mixture into it. Tilt pan back and forth to cover the bottom of the pan with egg mixture; as omelette cooks, draw edges toward center with a knife until the whole is set, pricking the soft spots with the tines of a fork to permit the top to set. Arrange mozzarella cheese on half the omelette, sprinkle with pepper (a little grated Parmesan cheese may be added), and carefully fold over the other half of the omelette. Bake in a preheated 350° F. oven until the cheese is melted. Serve sprinkled with parsley. You may also serve it with a tomato sauce. *Serves 4.*

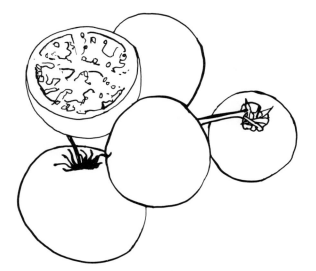

4
FISH

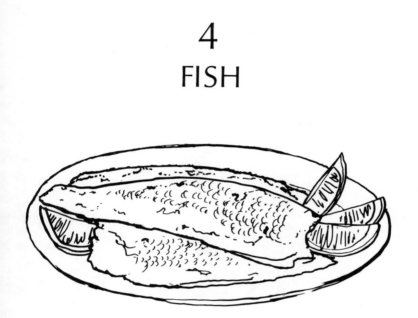

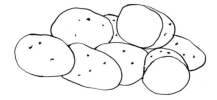

BAKED WHITE BASS WITH POTATOES IN
TOMATO SAUCE

2½ to 3 lbs. white bass
3 or 4 medium potatoes,
    cut into quarters
½ cup olive oil
1 cup dry white wine
1 16-oz. can tomatoes

2 tablespoons chopped
    parsley
1 clove garlic, minced
1 teaspoon oregano
salt and pepper

Parboil potatoes for about 8 minutes. Clean and wash fish; place in a deep baking pan. Arrange potatoes all around fish. Pour olive oil over fish and potatoes, rubbing oil well into fish. Pour wine over all. Drain tomatoes and, crushing between fingers, spread over fish. Combine parsley, garlic and oregano and sprinkle over all. Season with salt and pepper. Bake in moderate 350° F. oven for about 35 to 45 minutes, or until fish flakes easily to the fork and potatoes are done. *Serves 4.*

STUFFED BAKED CARP IN WHITE WINE

2½ to 3 lbs. carp
1 leek, chopped
2 tablespoons parsley, cut
   up
1 clove garlic, minced
3 slices French or Italian
   bread, diced, soaked
   in milk and drained

1 tablespoon olive oil
butter
olive oil
salt and pepper
dry white wine

Fish can be stuffed and baked with head and tail removed or not, as desired.

Clean fish, dry and rub inside and out with salt. Combine leek, parsley, garlic, bread and olive oil and toss lightly. Stuff fish with mixture and sew or skewer opening. Butter a glass baking pan and sprinkle with bread crumbs; place fish in pan. Dot fish with butter and brush with a little olive oil, season with salt and pepper and pour enough wine in pan to almost cover fish. Bake in hot 400° F. oven for about 15 minutes or until wine is reduced to almost half the amount. Lower temperature to 350° F. and bake 30 to 45 minutes longer. Baste often. Serve hot in glass baking pan. This recipe may be used for any other favorite baking fish, such as red snapper, bass, or bluefish. *Serves 4.*

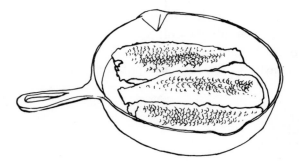

CLAM SOUP, NEAPOLITAN

24 small (littleneck) hard-
    shell clams
¼ cup olive oil
2 cloves garlic, minced
1 16-oz. can tomatoes
salt to taste
pinch of red pepper seeds
    or freshly ground
    black pepper

¼ teaspoon each oregano
    and basil
¼ cup dry white wine
    (optional)
1 tablespoon chopped
    parsley

A spicy Neapolitan first course that may be used as an entrée. Be sure to have plenty of crisp Italian or French bread on hand to dip in the sauce! And red wine is a "must" as beverage.

Scrub clams well under running water. Prepare sauce: brown garlic lightly in hot olive oil, add tomatoes, salt, pepper, oregano, basil and wine. Simmer for about 15 minutes or until sauce has thickened somewhat. Add the clams, mix, cover tightly and allow clams to steam open in the sauce, shaking pan occasionally. When clams are open (do not overcook) arrange them, shells and all, in soup dishes over a slice or two of toasted French or Italian bread; pour sauce over clams and sprinkle with parsley; serve immediately. Figure on 12 or more clams per serving. *Serves 2.*

SALTED COD, ROMAN STYLE

1½ to 2 lbs. soaked, boned,
    salted codfish (Bac-
    cala)
1 clove garlic, whole and
    crushed (optional)
1 medium onion, chopped
3 tablespoons olive oil

2 tablespoons tomato
    paste, dissolved in 1
    cup water
2 tablespoons pine nuts
2 tablespoons white seed-
    less raisins
freshly ground pepper

Cut codfish in squares or serving pieces. Brown garlic and onion in hot olive oil until onion is soft and transparent; remove garlic. Add dissolved tomato paste and simmer for about 5 minutes. Add codfish and season generously with pepper. Add pine nuts and raisins and simmer gently for about 20 to 30 minutes or until fish flakes easily with a fork and is tender. Taste for salt seasoning. Serve with Polenta (see page 201).

NOTE: for Neapolitan Baccala, cut codfish into squares, dip in flour and gently fry in olive oil. Drain on paper. Prepare sauce with 2 cloves of garlic, whole and crushed, browned in 3 tablespoons olive oil. Discard the garlic. Add dissolved tomato paste (same as above) and simmer 5 minutes. Add 1 tablespoon capers, 2 tablespoons pine nuts and ½ cup of pitted ripe olives and season with pepper. Arrange fried Baccala in a baking pan, pour sauce over, cover and bake in a preheated 375° F. oven for about 30 minutes. Taste for salt seasoning. *Serves 4.*

ROLLED FILLET OF FLOUNDER, PIQUANT

8 small fillets of flounder
1 teaspoon oregano
½ teaspoon dry mustard
dash of cayenne pepper
2 tablespoons chopped
   parsley
2 to 4 oz. anchovy fillets,
   mashed to a fine paste

2 tablespoons olive oil
1 tablespoon lemon juice
flour
1 or 2 eggs, lightly beaten
¼ cup olive oil
lemon wedges

Mix together well the oregano, mustard, cayenne pepper, parsley, anchovies, 2 tablespoons olive oil and lemon juice. Spread mixture on one side of flounder fillets and let stand for about a half hour. Roll up fillets and fasten with toothpicks. Roll first in flour, then dip in egg and fry gently in ¼ cup olive oil until brown and crisp. Arrange on serving dish, remove toothpicks and serve with lemon wedges. *Serves 4.*

FROGS' LEGS IN FRESH TOMATO SAUCE

16 pairs frogs' legs
milk, enough to cover
5 tablespoons butter
3 cloves garlic
2 tablespoons chopped
    parsley

4 ripe tomatoes, peeled
    and cut up
3 tablespoons olive oil
flour
salt and pepper to taste

Soak frogs' legs in milk for about 1 hour. Brown lightly 1 clove of garlic, whole and crushed, with 1 tablespoon of parsley in 3 tablespoons of butter; add the tomatoes. Season to taste and cook over high heat, stirring frequently, for about 15 to 20 minutes. Pat dry the frogs' legs and roll them in flour. Sauté them very quickly in a large skillet in hot olive oil and 2 tablespoons of butter with 2 cloves of garlic, minced, and 1 tablespoon of parsley (about 5 to 7 minutes). Pour tomato sauce over them and cook 2 to 3 minutes longer; serve. *Serves 4.*

MARINATED MIXED FISH FRY

3 fillets of flounder or any
    fish preferred, cut into
    large pieces
½ lb. shrimp, shelled and
    deveined
1 lb. small squid (optional)
½ lb. scallops
2 tablespoons parsley
1 clove garlic, minced
1 onion, minced

1 cup dry white wine
pinch of thyme
1 bay leaf, crushed

BATTER

3 eggs
1 cup flour
salt and pepper to taste
dry white wine, milk or
    water

A mixed fish fry is composed of different types of fish, dipped in batter, fried in deep fat or olive oil and served together. This recipe will give an exquisite flavor to what might otherwise be just an ordinary fish fry.

Prepare squid: Peel off thin skin from squid, remove insides along with cartilage or bone, severing tentacles from bodies. Remove eyes from tentacles. Cut body of squid into rings ½″ thick. Rinse rings and tentacles in cold water and dry thoroughly.

Prepare marinade: Combine parsley, garlic, onion, wine, thyme and bay leaf. Place all the fish in a bowl, pour marinade over all and toss, blending fish and marinade well. Let stand for about 1 hour. Prepare batter: beat eggs well, add flour gradually. Season with salt and pepper and add a little wine, milk or water to thin out if necessary. The batter should be thick but able to flow from a spoon easily. Remove fish from marinade and gently blot dry. Using a fork, dip pieces in the batter, lift and drain a little, then drop into deep hot fat or olive oil. Fry until each piece is a golden color and drain on absorbent paper. Keep warm. Serve hot, garnished with wedges of lemon. *Serves 4 to 6.*

LOBSTER ALL'AMERICANA

2 one-lb. lobsters	1 tablespoon tomato paste
½ cup olive oil	dissolved in 2 table-
½ onion, minced	spoons of water
½ stalk celery, minced	1 teaspoon butter
½ carrot, minced	1 oz. sweet cream
½ clove garlic, minced	1 teaspoon chopped
1 small bay leaf, crushed	parsley
2 jiggers cognac (2 oz.)	salt and pepper
1 cup dry white wine	

Be sure to buy live lobsters. Have large claws separated at the joints and cracked. Have tail separated from body and cut into 3 or 4 pieces, and the body split and cleaned. Brown the minced vegetables, garlic, and bay leaf in the olive oil in deep frying pan, then add the pieces of lobster. Cook over high heat, stirring well, until lobsters have turned a deep red. Drain as much of the oil as possible from pan, then moisten the lobster with cognac, raise flame, mix and add the wine. Add dissolved tomato paste, a pinch of salt and pepper. Cover and let cook for about 15 minutes. When done, arrange lobster pieces on serving dish and keep warm on back of stove. Prepare sauce by straining the contents of pan into a little saucepan; add butter and cream, mix and beat well over low heat until butter is melted and everything well blended. Do not boil. Pour over lobster, sprinkle with parsley. (Delicious served with rice.) *Serves 2.*

LOBSTER FRA DIAVOLO

2 live lobsters, medium size	1 tablespoon chopped parsley
3 cloves garlic, chopped	½ teaspoon salt
½ cup olive oil	⅛ teaspoon red pepper seeds
1 16-oz. can tomatoes	½ cup sherry or white wine
1 teaspoon oregano	

Have large claws of lobsters separated at the joints (leave them uncracked so as to retain all the juices). Have tail separated from body and cut into pieces; body split and cleaned. Brown garlic in olive oil, add tomatoes, and crush with fork. Add oregano, parsley, salt and red pepper (or black pepper if you prefer). Cook for a minute or two, then add sherry and let simmer for about 15 minutes. Add the lobster pieces and stir. Cover and let simmer for 20 minutes, or until lobster is cooked. Lobster shell will turn a deep red. Place lobster pieces in serving dish and pour sauce over all. (A few littleneck clams, washed and scrubbed, may be added during the last 5 minutes of cooking time.) *Serves 2.* (This sauce is delicious served on spaghetti.)

SHRIMP ALLA MARINARA

2 lbs. shrimp, shelled and deveined
¼ cup olive oil
2 cloves garlic, chopped
½ teaspoon oregano
1 16-oz. can tomatoes

1 tablespoon chopped parsley
½ teaspoon salt
pinch of red pepper seeds
½ cup sherry or sauterne

Lightly brown garlic with oregano in olive oil, add tomatoes, and crush with fork. Add parsley, salt and red pepper (or black pepper, if you prefer). Cook for a few minutes, then add the sherry and let simmer for about 15 minutes, or until somewhat thickened. Add shrimp, blend with sauce and let simmer for 15 to 20 minutes, or until shrimp are tender. Serve hot. Makes a delicious sauce for macaroni or spaghetti. *Serves 4.*

SHRIMP IN TOMATO AND WHITE WINE SAUCE

2 lbs. shrimp, shelled and deveined
½ cup flour
⅓ cup olive oil
½ cup Chablis
½ tablespoon tomato paste dissolved in ¼ cup warm water
½ teaspoon salt

dash cayenne pepper
1 tablespoon chopped parsley
1 small scallion, chopped
2 teaspoons lemon juice
triangle slices of bread fried in olive oil or toasted

Wash and dry shrimp. Roll in flour lightly and brown in hot oil in large frying pan. Drain oil from pan into a small saucepan, and set aside. Add wine to shrimp and cook until wine has evaporated almost completely. While wine is evaporating, add dissolved tomato paste to the oil in the saucepan, and simmer 3 to 4 minutes. Pour this mixture over shrimp after wine has evaporated, and season with salt and cayenne pepper. Mix parsley and chopped scallion together; stir into shrimp and let simmer for a few minutes. Remove pan from fire and add lemon juice. Arrange shrimp and sauce (which should be a bit thick) on serving dish, and garnish with triangular slices of fried or toasted bread. *Serves 4.*

STUFFED SQUID

8 small or 4 large squid	1 cup crumbed fresh
1 clove garlic, minced	bread
⅓ cup olive oil	salt and pepper to taste
1 tablespoon finely	¼ cup olive oil
chopped parsley	⅓ cup dry white wine
2 anchovy fillets,	
chopped fine	

Squid is also known as cuttlefish, poulpe and inkfish. (In Italian they are called calamai, calamari or sepie.) Once frowned upon by Americans, it has now become quite well-liked and is served in the finest Italian restaurants in this country. The following recipe is by far the most popular.

Peel off thin skin from squid; remove insides along with cartilage or bone, severing tentacles from bodies and keeping bodies whole. Discard eyes from tentacles; wash bodies and tentacles under running water, drain and pat dry. Chop tentacles very fine. Lightly brown garlic in ⅓ cup olive oil with parsley; add chopped tentacles and sauté for about 3 minutes; add anchovies, mix and blend thoroughly. Remove from heat; mix in the bread; taste for seasoning. (A little oregano or thyme may be added if you so desire.) Stuff squid bodies loosely (to allow for expansion) with this mixture and sew or fasten opening with toothpicks. Arrange stuffed squid in one layer in a baking pan, pour ¼ cup olive oil and the wine over them; sprinkle with salt and pepper, and bake covered in a preheated 350° F. oven for about 45 minutes or until tender, basting often. Serve with a little of the pan juice and wedges of lemon. These can also be baked in a favorite tomato sauce. *Serves 4.*

SQUID IN TOMATO SAUCE

1½ to 2 lbs. small squid	½ teaspoon oregano
1 medium onion, chopped fine	(optional)
2 cloves garlic, minced	1 tablespoon chopped parsley
¼ cup olive oil	¼ cup dry white wine
1 16-oz. can tomatoes, strained	(optional)
	salt and pepper to taste

Peel off thin skin from squid and remove insides along with cartilage or bone, severing tentacles from bodies. Discard eyes from tentacles; split tentacles in half; cut up bodies in large pieces. Wash pieces and tentacles under running water. Drain thoroughly. Lightly brown onion and garlic in olive oil; add tomatoes, oregano, parsley and wine; mix well. Simmer for about 10 minutes. Add cut up squid and tentacles. Season to taste (a tiny pinch of red pepper seeds may be added). Bring to a boil; lower heat, cover and simmer gently for about 2 to 2½ hours, depending upon the size of the squid. Remove cover the last few minutes of cooking time to reduce and thicken the sauce a little, if necessary. *Serves 4.*

FISH STEW, TUSCAN STYLE (Cacciucco)

1 sea bass or striped bass
1 lb. shrimp
1 dozen mussels or clams
1 crab or lobster
4 cloves garlic
½ teaspoon red pepper
    seeds
1 cup olive oil

1 cup Chablis or Bur-
    gundy
2 tablespoons tomato
    paste, dissolved in a
    little warm water
salt
Italian or French bread,
    sliced

*From the coast of the Tyrrhenian Sea comes this fish stew
(Cacciucco) . . . the popular fishermen's hearty fare, now
found on the menus of many elegant restaurants.*

Leave fish whole or cut into thick slices. Shell and devein
shrimp, leaving tails intact. Brush and clean mussels or clams
well. Break crab apart, or if you use lobster, cut into small
pieces. Place olive oil, 3 cloves of garlic chopped and pepper
in a Dutch oven and brown for a minute or two. Add wine and
dissolved tomato paste. Season slightly with salt and add bass,
shrimp, mussels and crab. Cover tightly and let cook undis-
turbed for about 30 minutes over a good heat, shaking pan
occasionally. Meanwhile toast bread (a good many slices)
and while still warm, rub with a clove of garlic. Arrange
bread in a deep serving dish, gently lift out fish from pan,
place on toast and pour pan sauce over all. Serve hot with
plenty of red wine as beverage. *Serves 4.*

STUFFED BAKED TROUT

4 fresh or frozen trout
    (one per serving)
8 anchovy fillets
8 tablespoons grated
    Parmesan cheese

salt and pepper to taste
dash of nutmeg
butter

Thaw frozen trout. Clean trout and wipe with a damp cloth. Mix 5 tablespoons grated cheese with salt, pepper and nutmeg. Stuff trout openings with this mixture and close with a toothpick or two. With a sharp knife make two diagonal gashes on each trout and stuff each gash with an anchovy fillet. Place trout in a well-buttered baking dish or pan, sprinkle with salt and pepper and the remaining grated cheese. Dot with butter. Bake in a preheated 350° F. oven for 30 to 40 minutes or until fish flakes easily to the fork. Serve with pan juices poured over trout, and with parsley potatoes. *Serves 4.*

BAKED WHITING WITH MUSHROOMS AND WINE

2 whitings (about 2 lbs.)
1 tablespoon butter
1 small onion, sliced fine
½ lb. mushrooms, sliced
salt and pepper
2 tablespoons grated
    Parmesan cheese,
    mixed with 2 table-
    spoons bread crumbs

½ cup dry white wine
¼ cup melted butter
1 teaspoon chopped
    parsley
lemon juice

Clean and split fish. Generously butter a baking dish or pan. Arrange onions in bottom of baking dish and top with mushrooms. Place fish on mushrooms, skin side up and split side under, in reverse (head-tail) positions. Pour melted butter over fish. Sprinkle with salt, pepper, and mixture of cheese and bread crumbs. Pour wine all around fish in the bottom of pan. Bake in hot oven (400° F.) for about 15 or 20 minutes. Before serving, sprinkle with chopped parsley and squeeze lemon juice over all. Serve hot. *Serves 2 to 4.*

SAVORY STEAMED WHITING

4 small whitings (one per serving)	¼ cup minced onion (optional)
flour	¼ cup dry white wine
salt and pepper to taste	2 tablespoons chopped parsley
½ cup olive oil	
4 cloves garlic, crushed	juice of half a lemon

Whiting (Merluzzo) has a delicate white flesh and is deliciously flavored. It needs gentle handling and cooks in just a few minutes. And, best of all, it is inexpensive in this country because of its abundance. The Italians call this dish "Merluzzo in Brodetto."

Clean fish and wipe dry. Roll lightly in flour. Lightly sauté onion and garlic in olive oil until onion is softened (do not brown). Add whitings and sauté for a minute or two, turning gently. Add wine, sprinkle with salt and freshly ground pepper; cover tightly and allow fish to steam gently in this savory liquid until tender, shaking pan occasionally. Whitings should be watched carefully, as their delicate flesh cooks quickly. Gently lift from pan and place each whiting in a soup dish. Add parsley and lemon juice to pan liquid, raise heat and simmer for a few seconds. Discard garlic, pour sauce over each fish and serve. (Sauce [brodetto] is rather soupy.) Serve with plenty of French or Italian bread. *Serves 4.* (For added color ½ teaspoon tomato paste may be added, dissolved in the white wine.)

5
POULTRY

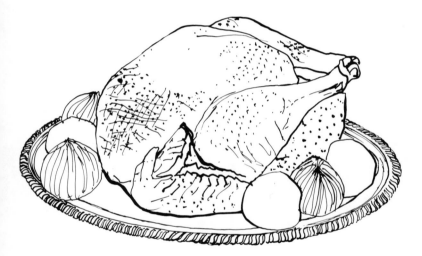

STUFFED CAPON, GOURMET

3 to 4 lb. whole boiled
    capon (or chicken)
½ cup butter
1½ tablespoons flour
2 cups hot milk
pinch of nutmeg
½ teaspoon salt
¼ teaspoon pepper
½ lb. elbow macaroni,
    cooked

2 cups mozzarella,
    gruyere or Swiss
    cheese, diced or
    grated
boiled liver, heart and
    gizzard, chopped
5 tablespoons grated
    Parmesan cheese

A festive treatment of boiled capon.

With a sharp pointed knife, very carefully make an incision through skin and meat of capon along the center of breast from neck to vent, and an incision on each side from wing to second joint. Gently loosen meat from breastbone, running knife underneath so as to remove the breast meat intact in two large solid pieces. With poultry shears or sharp kitchen scissors, cut away the bared breastbone so as to leave a large cavity. Melt butter in saucepan, blend in flour and add milk gradually, stirring constantly, until sauce starts to thicken. This sauce should not be too thick. Just before removing from fire, stir in nutmeg, salt and pepper. Mix macaroni with half of the white sauce; add the chopped-up liver, heart and gizzard, the mozarella cheese, 3 tablespoons of grated cheese and mix well. Stuff the large cavity of the capon, pressing in the macaroni mixture and heaping it in a dome shape so as to assume the likeness of the missing breastbone. Smooth the macaroni and then arrange the large slices of breast meat on top, so that capon assumes its original form. Tie and place capon in shallow, buttered baking pan. Reheat the remaining white sauce, adding 2 tablespoons of grated cheese. Pour over the capon. Bake in hot 400° F. oven until capon acquires a golden brown coating. *Serves 4 to 6.*

BAKED CHICKEN IN SAVORY CRUMBS

1 broiler-fryer, about 2½
   to 3 lbs., cut up
½ cup butter, melted
½ cup bread crumbs
¼ teaspoon salt
⅛ teaspoon pepper

⅛ teaspoon each garlic
   powder, onion
   powder, sage,
   marjoram and thyme
1 teaspoon chopped
   parsley
¼ teaspoon paprika

So simple—so quick . . . and the result is deliciously crisp fried-like chicken.

Arrange chicken pieces, skin side up, in a shallow baking dish close together. Pour melted butter over chicken. Combine bread crumbs with the rest of ingredients except paprika, mix well and sprinkle mixture over chicken, covering it well. Sprinkle with paprika. Bake uncovered in a preheated, 350° F. oven for about 1 hour or until tender. *Serves 4.*

BAKED CHICKEN IN BATTER, PIEDMONT

2½ to 3 lb. broiler,
   quartered

MARINADE

⅓ cup olive oil
juice of 1 lemon
½ small onion, minced
2 tablespoons minced
   parsley
salt and pepper to taste

BATTER

2 egg yolks
⅔ cup water
2 tablespoons olive oil
1 tablespoon grated
   Parmesan cheese
1 cup flour
½ teaspoon salt
2 egg whites, beaten stiff

A delicious preparation—marinated chicken, coated with a tasty batter and then baked to a brown crispness.

Place chicken in a bowl; combine marinade ingredients and

pour over chicken; rub into each piece. Let stand for 2 hours or more, turning pieces occasionally. *Prepare Batter*: Beat egg yolks until thick and lemon colored; add water, olive oil, cheese, flour and salt. Blend well. Fold in egg whites. Lift chicken pieces from marinade, dip in batter, coating well, and arrange in one layer in a greased baking pan. Bake in preheated 425° F. oven about 45 minutes, turning pieces once. *Serves 4.*

CHEESE-BAKED CHICKEN BREASTS
WITH BROCCOLI

2 whole chicken breasts
1 or 2 eggs, slightly
    beaten
flour
salt and pepper
2 tablespoons butter
2 tablespoons olive oil
4 slices prosciutto or
    boiled ham

4 slices mozzarella, Swiss
    cheese or Fontina
1 bunch broccoli
¼ cup chicken bouillon
⅓ cup melted butter
grated Parmesan cheese

Split breasts in half; bone and skin. Pound chicken pieces thin between 2 sheets of wax paper. Dip chicken in beaten eggs, then dredge in flour seasoned with salt and pepper. Sauté chicken in a mixture of two tablespoons butter and 2 tablespoons olive oil until tender and lightly colored on both sides. Meanwhile cook broccoli in a small quantity of boiling salted water until tender, about 8 to 10 minutes. Drain. Arrange broccoli spears in one layer in a baking dish; pour melted butter over them and sprinkle with grated cheese. Place chicken pieces on top of broccoli; top each chicken piece with a slice of prosciutto and cover with a slice of mozzarella. Pour bouillon over all. Cover and bake in a preheated 375° F. oven for about 15 to 20 minutes. Serve immediately. *Serves 4.*

BONED CHICKEN BREASTS WITH
RICE AND MUSHROOMS

⅔ cup rice
9 tablespoons butter (1
    stick + 1 tablespoon)
2 tablespoons grated
    Parmesan cheese
1 egg yolk
2 chicken breasts, split
¼ cup Marsala or sherry
    wine
1 or 2 eggs beaten
    slightly

½ lb. fresh mushrooms or
    canned sliced
    mushrooms
1 tablespoon chopped
    parsley
1 teaspoon lemon juice
flour
bread crumbs
salt and pepper to taste

A grand duke from the ancient royal house of Piedmont was responsible for these delicious chicken breasts elegantly served on rice cakes and smothered with mushrooms . . . "alla Granduca."

Cook rice in boiling salted water until tender; drain, and while still hot stir into it thoroughly 1 tablespoon butter, grated cheese and the egg yolk and let cool. With sharp knife carefully remove bones from chicken breasts. Dredge each breast in flour and sauté gently in 3 tablespoons of hot butter, moistening with Marsala, a little at a time, and seasoning with salt and pepper. Cook until tender and golden brown. Meanwhile divide rice into 4 balls and flatten each into an oval-shaped patty about the size of the chicken breasts. Dip each patty in beaten egg, then roll in bread crumbs and brown in 2 tablespoons of hot butter. While chicken and rice patties are browning, sauté mushrooms in 3 tablespoons of butter; add parsley, season with salt, pepper and lemon juice. Arrange rice patties on warm serving dish, top each with a chicken breast and cover with sautéed mushrooms. *Serves 4.*

CHICKEN CACCIATORA (HUNTER STYLE)

2½ to 3 lb. broiler, cut into small pieces
3 tablespoons olive oil
¼ cup chopped onion
1 teaspoon chopped parsley
1 16-oz. can whole peeled tomatoes

1 teaspoon salt
1 dash pepper
1 teaspoon dried basil leaves, or sprig of fresh basil
¼ cup sherry, or white or red wine

Heat oil slightly in deep frying pan or casserole, add chicken and brown until golden on all sides; then add onion, parsley, basil, salt and pepper. Brown together with chicken until onion is almost golden, then pour wine over chicken. Cover. Let simmer for a minute or so, then add tomatoes. Cover, and simmer for 20 to 30 minutes or until chicken is tender. *Serves 4.*

CHICKEN FLAMBÉ

2½ to 3 lb. broiler, cut into serving pieces
¼ cup olive oil
salt and pepper to taste
dash each of thyme and marjoram
1 teaspoon wine vinegar
⅛ lb. prosciutto or ham, cut into slivers

2 carrots, sliced in thin rounds
2 medium onions, sliced thin
2 bay leaves
2 cloves
1 clove garlic, minced
½ cup dry white wine
¼ cup brandy, heated

For an exciting dinner-party effect . . . before adding the cognac, and for the last few minutes of cooking time, transfer to a warmed chafing dish, continue cooking, and with a flair add the brandy and ignite!

45

Season each piece of chicken in a mixture of salt, pepper, thyme and marjoram. Brown in very hot olive oil, turning often, to brown evenly. Add vinegar and all the remaining ingredients except brandy. Cover and cook over a moderate heat for about 40 to 45 minutes, turning chicken once or twice only. Add more wine or a little bouillon if needed. When ready to serve, pour brandy into pan, set it aflame, and serve at once. *Serves 4.*

CHICKEN, HUNTER STYLE, WITH OLIVES

2½ to 3 lb. broiler	2 tablespoons chopped
1 cup white wine (dry	parsley
or sweet)	2 cloves garlic
salt and pepper	8 oz. ripe olives, pitted
½ teaspoon ginger	toast triangles rubbed
¼ lb. salt pork	with garlic

Have chicken cut in very small pieces. Wash and dry thoroughly. Place chicken pieces in skillet, add wine and cook over high heat, adding ¼ cup water. Season with salt, pepper and ginger. Meanwhile chop salt pork in wooden bowl together with garlic and parsley. When liquid in skillet is almost absorbed add the salt pork mixture, mixing and blending well with chicken, maintaining high heat, so as to thoroughly brown pieces of chicken. When chicken is well-colored, add the olives, lower heat and continue cooking for a few minutes longer or until chicken is tender. Serve on toasted garlic bread. *Serves 4.*

CHICKEN LIVERS WITH SAGE

1 lb. chicken livers, each
    liver cut in 2 or 3
    pieces
¼ cup butter
¼ teaspoon salt
⅛ teaspoon pepper
1 teaspoon chopped sage
    leaves

2 slices prosciutto or lean
    bacon, cut into slivers
4 slices bread, cut in
    triangles and fried in
    butter
½ cup Marsala or sherry
1 tablespoon butter

Melt the ¼ cup butter in shallow pan, add chicken livers, salt, pepper, sage and prosciutto and cook about 5 minutes. Remove livers from pan and place in warm serving dish on fried bread triangles. Add wine to pan juices, mix well and cook 3 minutes. Add 1 tablespoon butter, mix well and pour over livers and fried bread. *Serves 4.*

MARINATED FRIED CHICKEN, FLORENTINE

1 or 2 small broilers
3 tablespoons butter
2 small onions, minced
1 stalk celery, minced
2 carrots, minced
2 cloves
5 peppercorns
½ teaspoon each
    rosemary, sage and
    basil

2 cups white vinegar
2 cups dry white wine
2 or 3 eggs, slightly
    beaten
flour
bread crumbs
olive oil for deep frying

An exquisite manner of preparing fried chicken.

Brown the vegetables with cloves, peppercorns and herbs in butter until softened and golden colored. Add vinegar and wine, bring to a boil and let simmer until reduced to half the amount; cool. Meanwhile prepare chicken: cut in quarters; remove breastbones, leaving the second wing bone; remove thigh bone and leave drumstick. Pound quarters lightly. Arrange the quartered chicken in a large, deep platter or casserole, pour over chicken the cold browned vegetable and wine mixture, covering each piece, and let marinate for about 3 hours. One-half hour before serving, lift chicken quarters from marinade, blot dry, dredge in flour, dip in egg and then in bread crumbs. Fry in deep hot olive oil over moderate heat until tender and golden brown. Drain on paper and serve. *Serves 4.*

CHICKEN WITH PROSCIUTTO AND MUSHROOMS

2 to 3 lb. broiler or fryer, cut in small serving pieces
1 cup flour
3 tablespoons olive oil
salt and pepper
¼ lb. prosciutto, cut in slivers

1 bay leaf
1 clove garlic (optional)
½ lb. fresh mushrooms, cleaned and cut up
½ cup dry white wine
1 16-oz. can tomatoes, drained and cut up

Wash, drain and thoroughly dry chicken. Dust pieces in flour. Brown pieces of chicken thoroughly in hot oil and butter and season with salt and pepper. When chicken is well browned, add cut-up prosciutto, bay leaf, garlic and mushrooms. Continue cooking for about 3 minutes. Add wine and let evaporate, then add tomatoes. Cook for about 15 to 20 minutes longer over high heat until chicken is tender. *Serves 4.*

BEEF AND SPINACH STUFFED ROAST CHICKEN

4 lb. roasting chicken	2 eggs, slightly beaten
1 lb. chopped beef, or	2 tablespoons grated
½ lb. each chopped	Parmesan cheese
veal and beef	salt and pepper
½ onion, minced fine	dash nutmerg (optional)
2 tablespoons butter	olive oil
1 lb. fresh spinach, or 1	4 med. potatoes, pared
package frozen	and quartered
spinach	

A popular Tuscan dressing for chicken.

Wash and clean chicken and remove neck, leaving skin. Rub neck and body cavities with salt. Cook spinach only until barely tender; don't overcook. Drain thoroughly until dry and chop fine. Brown meat and onion in hot butter until onion is golden colored and juices from meat have evaporated. Remove from fire, add spinach, eggs, cheese, salt and pepper to taste, and nutmeg. Mix and blend thoroughly. Fill neck cavity of chicken and fasten neck skin to body with skewer, or tie in place. Fill body cavity with stuffing loosely, allowing for expansion. Close incision with skewers and lace together with cord, wrapping this cord around end of legs and tying securely to tail piece, so legs are close to body. Pour a little olive oil all over chicken. Place in roasting pan in preheated 325° F. oven, uncovered, basting with pan drippings. Figure on 20 to 30 minutes per pound, according to age of fowl. 45 minutes before fowl is done, put potatoes around chicken in pan and roast with chicken until both are done. For a delightful flavor, I sprinkle chicken and potatoes with a little rosemary and garlic powder while roasting. *Serves 4 to 6.*

CHICKEN STEW WITH ROSEMARY

2½ to 3 lb. broiler, cut into small serving pieces
¾ cup olive oil
2 cloves garlic, chopped fine
2 teaspoons rosemary, crushed

salt and pepper
½ cup dry white wine
2 tablespoons tomato paste, dissolved in ¼ cup warm water

A variation of the popular "Cacciatora" is this stew, the famous "Potacchio" from the Marches of Italy on the Adriatic.

Brown chicken in hot olive oil in large, deep frying pan, until golden colored. Add garlic and rosemary and continue browning chicken until well-colored. Sprinkle with salt and pepper. Add wine, mix and let simmer for a minute or two. Add dissolved tomato paste, and mix everything together well. Lower flame to moderate heat and continue cooking slowly until chicken pieces are tender and well-coated with sauce. The sauce should not be abundant—the chicken pieces should be well-glazed with sauce. After adding the dissolved tomato paste, the chicken can be baked in a preheated 350° F. oven for about 15 to 20 minutes to obtain this glazed result. *Serves 4.*

DUCK, PALERMO STYLE

3 or 4 lb. duck
1 tablespoon butter
2 tablespoons olive oil
⅛ lb. lean unsalted pork
lard or bacon,
chopped
pinch of thyme
1 bay leaf
1 clove garlic, minced
½ cup sauterne, sherry or
Marsala
½ cup wine vinegar
(red)
salt and pepper

1 teaspoon tomato paste
dissolved in ½ cup
water
1 lb. small white onions
2 cups green olives,
pitted
grated rind of 1 lemon
grated rind of 1 orange
1 teaspoon Worcestershire
sauce
3 thin slices of orange,
halved
1 jigger cognac (1½ oz.)

Sicily is the birthplace of this succulent duck, ringed with onions and olives, garnished with orange slices and spiked with cognac! . . . and the drained fat from the pan will make the most delicious fried potatoes.

Peel and cook onions 10 minutes in boiling water to which 2 tablespoons of vinegar have been added. Drain and set aside. Wash duck in cold water and dry well; cut into serving pieces. In a large deep frying pan or casserole brown duck in olive oil, butter and lean unsalted pork lard; adding thyme, bay leaf, garlic. Brown, turning pieces often, until each has acquired a nice golden color. Drain all but about 2 or 3 tablespoons of fat from the pan. Pour over the duck the wine and vinegar, season with salt and pepper, and continue cooking over high heat until wine and vinegar have evaporated. Stir in dissolved tomato paste, and cover. Cook over moderate heat for about 45 minutes, adding a little water if sauce becomes too thick. Then add onions, olives, grated lemon and orange rind, Worcestershire sauce; mix everything well together and cook 15 minutes longer. Arrange duck pieces on warm platter, surround with the onions and olives, pouring pan sauce over all. Decorate top with halved orange slices. Drizzle the cognac over all and garnish platter with slices of white bread fried in olive oil. Serve immediately. *Serves 4.*

PÂTÉ STUFFED DUCK

4 to 6 lb. duckling
½ lb. veal liver, chopped fine
4 tablespoons butter
1 cup bread crumbs
⅓ cup grated Parmesan cheese
1 egg
⅛ teaspoon ground clove

1 teaspoon sage
pinch of nutmeg
warm broth or chicken bouillon
salt and pepper
⅛ lb. prosciutto, cut in small pieces
1 lb. small onions
½ cup Burgundy

You can substitute chicken livers for the veal liver.

In a small frying pan sauté liver in about 1 tablespoon of butter until cooked; chop, mash or pass through a food chopper. In a bowl mix together the liver, cheese, egg, ground clove, nutmeg, sage and bread crumbs. Stirring constantly, gradually add just enough broth to make a smooth thick mixture. Add salt to taste. Tie back the duck's neck skin, stuff the duck with the mixture and sew the opening tightly or use skewers. Place duck on a rack in a shallow baking pan, sprinkle with prosciutto and season with salt and pepper. (Do not cover, or add water, or baste.) For medium-well-done, cook 18 minutes per pound, and for very-well-done, 22 to 25 minutes per pound. In the meantime, clean and wash onions, boil them until half-cooked, and drain. A half hour before duck is done, add the wine, and place half-cooked onions in bottom of pan all around duck. To serve, scoop stuffing from duck and place in center of serving dish; cut duck into serving pieces, arrange pieces on top of stuffing and then surround with onions. *Serves 4.*

DUCK IN SALMI

1 medium-sized duck,
    cut in pieces
liver, heart and gizzard,
    chopped fine
1 large onion
3 cloves
1 teaspoon sage

1 bay leaf
salt and pepper to taste
¼ cup olive oil
1 cup dry white wine
1 cup sherry
2 sheets brown paper
slices of toasted bread

Salmi is a ragout of game or fowl, stewed in wine . . . keep the lid on tightly while cooking. The pan juices may be thickened as for gravy, if you so desire. For a perfect effect serve with egg noodles or rice.

Skin duck. With sharp, pointed knife, cut through duck skin along center of breast from neck to vent, then along backbone. Loosen skin by pulling away from flesh, at the same time running knife underneath, close to flesh. Peel skin back as it is loosened. (You can have your poultry dealer do this for you.) Cut duck in serving pieces. In a heavy saucepan or Dutch oven, place the onion (whole) spiked with the cloves; add the sage, bay leaf, chopped liver, heart and gizzard, and the pieces of duck. Sprinkle with salt and pepper, pour over all the oil, white wine and sherry. Cover pan with a double sheet of brown paper. Cover and cook very slowly over a moderate heat until done, about 18 to 20 minutes to the pound (do not uncover—shake pan occasionally). When done, remove pieces of duck and place on toasted bread on serving dish. Strain pan juices, skim fat off with spoon or paper napkin, and pour over duck and toast. *Serves 4.*

SQUABS IN FOIL

2 pigeon squabs, or
    small chicken squabs
5 tablespoons butter
salt and pepper
½ cup dry white wine
½ cup bouillon
2 scallions, minced

1 onion, minced
2 tablespoons olive oil
½ lb. mushrooms, sliced
1 tablespoon ·chopped
    parsley
8 thin slices prosciutto
    or ham

These delicious squabs may be prepared in advance, either in the morning or the day before, wrapped in foil, refrigerated and then baked just before serving. If they are prepared in advance be sure to remove them from refrigerator at least an hour before baking. Try them on your charcoal grill!

Split squabs in two, pound to flatten out and break up bones. Remove breast and backbones. Brown halves on both sides in a large skillet in 3 tablespoons of butter, seasoning with salt and pepper. Moisten with wine while browning and let wine evaporate. Then add bouillon, lower heat and let simmer until tender, turning often. Remove from pan and let cool. Meanwhile lightly brown scallions and onions in 2 tablespoons butter and olive oil, add mushrooms and sauté until tender (about 5 to 7 minutes). Stir in parsley and cook for a few seconds more. Cool. Cut aluminum foil into 4 large rounds. Place a slice of prosciutto on each round, off center, top with a little mushroom mixture, arrange squab half on top, then top with more mushroom mixture and cover with another slice of prosciutto. Fold foil over in half-moon shape, and crimp edges. Place on a baking sheet and bake in a preheated 350° F. oven for about 30 minutes. Serve hot in foil. *Serves 4.*

STUFFED TURKEY, LOMBARDY

For a 10 lb. turkey:

STUFFING

½ lb. chopped beef
½ lb. sweet Italian sausage, skinned and chopped
3 eggs
½ cup bread crumbs
¼ cup grated Parmesan cheese
salt and pepper
¼ teaspoon nutmeg
¼ lb. pitted prunes, cut up
2 small apples, peeled and cut into small pieces
15 boiled chestnuts, peeled and broken up
heart, liver and gizzard, cut up
¼ cup chopped lean unsalted pork lard, prosciutto, ham or bacon
½ cup dry white wine

INGREDIENTS FOR ROASTING

½ cup butter
2 slices prosciutto
2 slices salt pork
½ teaspoon sage
½ teaspoon rosemary
1 cup dry white wine
hot broth, stock or water
2 tablespoons flour

The succulence of this turkey is due to the flavor harmony of the ingredients in the dressing.

Combine and mix all ingredients for stuffing. Fill neck cavity loosely with stuffing and fasten neck skin flat to back with skewer or cord. Fold wing tips up toward back, tying in place if necessary. Fill body cavity loosely with stuffing, allowing for expansion. Close incision by inserting skewers across opening and lacing together with cord, then wrap cord around legs and tie securely to tail piece, so legs are close to body. Place slices of prosciutto, salt pork, sage and rosemary in bottom of well-buttered shallow roasting pan. Rub remaining butter all over turkey and place in pan. Place pan on top of stove over high heat, sear on all sides until browned to a golden color, or place under hot broiler and brown well on all sides. Remove from stove top or broiler. Pour wine over turkey and place in preheated 325° F. oven. Roast uncovered until tender (allow 25 minutes per lb.), basting often, moistening with a little hot broth or wine occasionally. When half-done, season with salt and pepper. Remove string and skewers before serving.

GRAVY

Place 2 tablespoons flour in a cup, mix with a little water or white wine, add a few spoonfuls of the drippings from pan, then stir into rest of drippings in pan and cook over heat until smooth. Pass through fine strainer into gravy bowl or boat. Serve hot with turkey.

6
MEATS

Beef

BEEF SLICES, PIZZAIOLA

1 to 1½ lb. thin strips top
    or bottom round
    chuck or sirloin tip
⅓ cup olive oil

1 clove garlic, minced
½ 16-oz. can tomatoes
½ teaspoon oregano
salt and pepper

Pound slices of beef well. Brown meat in olive oil quickly on both sides. Remove meat, set aside, and keep warm. Brown garlic in hot olive oil in which meat has been browned, add tomatoes, oregano, salt and pepper. Mix and crush tomatoes with fork and cook for about 10 minutes over high heat. Return meat slices to pan with sauce. Cook in sauce first on one side, then on the other, until tender or to desired doneness. Arrange meat on serving dish and pour sauce over it. *Serves 4.*

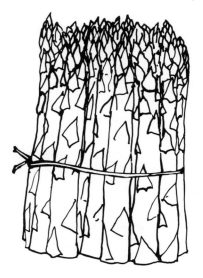

BOILED BEEF IN CASSEROLE WITH VEGETABLES

1 lb. small new potatoes
¼ cup olive oil
½ lb. shelled peas or 1 can peas
1½ cups dried mushrooms, soaked in warm water
1 tablespoon olive oil
1 16-oz. can tomatoes
⅛ lb. lean bacon, diced very small
2 tablespoons butter
2 tablespoons flour

¼ cup dry white wine
2 cups broth, beef bouillon or water
1½ lbs. cold boiled beef, sliced thin
4 boiled carrots, cut in ¼" rounds
½ lb. small onions (4 to 6), boiled
6 to 8 celery stalks, cut in two and boiled
½ cup grated Parmesan cheese

If your family frowns upon boiled beef after enjoying the soup, this homey casserole with its vegetables is the solution. You can also substitute any leftover cooked meats or fowl for the boiled beef.

Peel and dice potatoes and sauté gently in ¼ cup olive oil, sprinkle with salt, and cook until tender and nicely colored. Cook fresh peas in a little salted water with a lump of butter and drain; or, if canned peas, drain and sauté for a minute or two in a little butter. Drain mushrooms after soaking for ½ hour and sauté them in 1 tablespoon of olive oil, seasoning with a little salt. Drain tomatoes, reserve juice, and crush tomatoes a little. Prepare a sauce by searing the bacon gently in 2 tablespoons of butter; stir in flour, mix well and add the wine, broth and juice from drained tomatoes; stirring constantly, cook until sauce starts to thicken and remove from heat. Generously grease a casserole or baking pan with butter. Place a layer of sliced beef, then a layer each of the various vegetables and potatoes already prepared, and the tomatoes. Sprinkle with plenty of grated cheese. Repeat this procedure until meat and vegetables are all used, ending with a top layer of vegetables and grated cheese. Pour sauce over all. Cover and bake in moderate oven (375° F.) for 30 minutes. Serve hot from casserole. *Serves 4 to 6.*

EGG STUFFED BEEF ROLL, SICILIAN STYLE

1 large slice top round of
  beef, ½" thick
3 slices bread, crust
  removed
1 small onion, minced
½ lb. ground veal
½ lb. sweet Italian
  sausages
pinch of nutmeg
½ teaspoon oregano
2 eggs, slightly beaten
2 tablespoons Marsala
  or sherry
6 slices bacon

1 tablespoon grated
  Parmesan cheese
½ cup cooked peas
½ cup diced cooked
  carrots
4 hard-cooked eggs
¼ cup olive oil
2 tablespoons butter
2 stalks celery, cut up
2 carrots, sliced
1 onion, sliced thin
1 teaspoon basil
½ cup dry white wine
¼ cup Marsala or sherry

The work involved in preparing this roll is well worth it—when sliced it is a work of art, and a gourmet's delight. Have slice of beef butterflied so as to have a large piece of meat; pound uncut edge flat. Flank steak may be used, split lengthwise with grain, almost in two; open and pound uncut edge flat; steak is now half as thick and twice as wide.

Cut a thin slice from each end of hard-cooked eggs so they can be placed together in a row. Soak bread in a little milk and squeeze dry. Lightly brown minced onion in a little butter until softened. Remove casings from sausages. Combine sausage meat, ground veal, browned onion and bread. Mix and blend well or pass through food chopper. Add nutmeg, oregano, salt and pepper to taste, and bind with beaten eggs. Stir in Marsala. Carefully pound slice of meat until thin but still intact. Spread surface with ⅓ of the meat mixture, cover with slices of bacon. Add to the remaining meat mixture the grated cheese, cooked peas and carrots, mixing gently, and place in a heap lengthwise on top of bacon in center of slice of meat. Arrange hard-cooked eggs side by side in a row on top of mixture, pressing them down so that they are all covered by the mixture, and then roll slice of meat. Wrap roll in a damp-

61

ened piece of cheesecloth and tie securely with string so that it resembles a large salami. Place olive oil, butter, sliced carrots, celery, onion, and basil in baking casserole and arrange roll on top. Bake in preheated 400° F. oven for 30 minutes, turning often, moisten with white wine and Marsala, reduce temperature to 350° F. and continue cooking slowly for about another hour, turning occasionally. When done, lift roll from pan and rest in warm place for about 20 minutes before removing cheesecloth. Slice and serve with pan sauce. *Serves 4 to 6.*

FILLET OF BEEF IN MARSALA AND COGNAC

2 lbs. tenderloin of beef,
    in one piece
3 slices prosciutto, cut
    up in slivers
1½ cups Marsala or sherry
1 jigger cognac
salt and pepper to taste
½ stalk celery, minced
½ teaspoon chopped
    parsley

3 tablespoons butter
1 small onion, minced
1 small carrot, minced
½ stalk celery, minced
1 teaspoon chopped
    parsley
¼ cup of stock, broth or
    bouillon
1 teaspoon flour
1 teaspoon butter

Have butcher tie meat to hold shape. Lard meat by making cuts in it with thin, sharp knife and inserting pieces of prosciutto, using all of them. Place meat in deep dish and pour over it Marsala and cognac. Add salt, pepper, celery, and parsley and let stand about 12 hours in refrigerator, turning frequently. When ready to cook, remove meat from marinade, strain marinade; pat meat dry, and place in heavy deep skillet or Dutch oven with butter, onion, celery, carrot and parsley, and brown thoroughly on all sides. When meat and vegetables are thoroughly browned, add 1 cup of strained marinade and sear for another 15 or 20 minutes, so that meat is well browned on the outside and rare on the inside. Remove meat and place on dish to keep warm, and prepare gravy. Add ¼ cup of stock to juices in pan, scraping sides and bottom; stirring constantly, add flour, let cook rapidly until it starts to thicken, remove from heat. Add 1 teaspoon butter, blend until melted. Strain gravy. Remove string from meat, cut in thick slices, reshape on serving dish and pour gravy over it. *Serves 4.*

LITTLE FILLETS OF BEEF, NEAPOLITAN

1 to 1½ lbs. tenderloin of beef, cut in ¼″ thick slices	1 oz. dry mushrooms
	2 tablespoons chopped parsley
butter	salt and pepper
3 or 4 slices prosciutto, chopped	juice of half a lemon
	2 or 3 tablespoons broth

A quick, gala entrée. Thin club steaks, boned and trimmed, heart steaks or slices from the eye of rib may be substituted for the tenderloin of beef.

Soak mushrooms in 1 cup of warm water until softened. Drain and chop. Butter well the bottom of a large, shallow frying pan. Sprinkle the chopped prosciutto evenly in bottom of pan, and place over prosciutto the chopped mushrooms, topping with the chopped parsley. Arrange the meat slices on top, in one layer, season with salt and pepper and place over moderate heat. When browned on one side, turn each slice gently so that some of chopped mixture may adhere to meat, and let brown on other side. When browned on both sides, sprinkle lemon juice over each slice of meat, add 2 or 3 tablespoons of broth to pan and, raising heat, finish cooking until tender and of desired doneness. Place on hot serving dish, pour pan sauce over all and serve. *Serves 4.*

ROAST MARINATED FILLET OF BEEF

½ to 1 whole fillet or
    tenderloin of beef
small strips of fat salt pork
1½ cup Burgundy
¼ cup tarragon vinegar
dash each of thyme,
    nutmeg and cloves
2 cloves garlic, crushed
1 bay leaf, crumbled
1 onion, thinly sliced

½ lemon, thinly sliced
1 carrot, chopped
2 tablespoons each
    minced onion and
    carrots
3 tablespoons butter
3 tablespoons flour
1 cup beef bouillon
6 peppercorns
salt

*This is a king's offering for a V.I.P. dinner. When buying a
fillet or tenderloin of beef, figure on at least ½ lb. per serving.
A good fillet should be well browned on the outside and rare
or medium rare on the inside.*

Have fillet of beef trimmed. Lard with the strips of salt pork.
Place in a deep dish, sprinkle with salt. Combine the seasonings, garlic, bay leaf, sliced onion, lemon slices and chopped
carrot with the wine and vinegar and pour over meat. Cover
and marinate for about 12 hours, turning meat every 3 or 4
hours. Lift meat from marinade and blot dry; reserve the
marinade. Rub fillet with butter and salt and pepper to taste.
Roast in a shallow pan in a hot 450° F. oven for 25 to 35 minutes, depending upon size of fillet. Baste frequently with a little of the marinade for the first 10 minutes, then with the
juices from the pan. Meanwhile prepare a sauce with the marinade: brown minced onion and carrots in butter; stir in flour
and let brown. Add 1 cup of beef bouillon, mixed with 1 cup
of the drained marinade. Add peppercorns and salt to taste.
Cook, stirring constantly until sauce is smooth and starts to
thicken. Strain through a fine sieve. Return to heat and keep
warm. Arrange roast on heated platter, slice enough portions
to go around once and reshape. Pour part of sauce over slices
of roasted fillet, serve rest for individual helpings. *Serves 6 to 8.*

HUNGARIAN BEEF GOULASH

3 lbs. beef chuck, cut into
    1½″ cubes for stew
2 tablespoons olive oil
1½ large yellow onions,
    chopped
3 tablespoons paprika

3 large fresh tomatoes,
    peeled and cut up
    coarsely
3 green peppers, cut up
    coarsely
salt and pepper
egg noodles, cooked

Goulash "Gulyas": a thick meat stew of Hungarian origin.

In a heavy deep pan or Dutch oven heat the olive oil, add the onions and sauté slowly until very soft. Gradually blend in paprika. Add beef; raise heat and brown meat lightly, stirring it constantly with a wooden spoon. Add tomatoes, with juice, and peppers. Season with salt and pepper to taste. Cover pan tightly. Lower heat and simmer slowly for 2 hours. Shake pan to prevent scorching, but do not remove cover to stir. By that time the juices from the vegetables and meat will have risen so meat is covered. The meat in a goulash should be very soft and almost falling to pieces. Goulash "gulyas" is even better reheated than when freshly cooked. Serve with cooked noodles. *Serves 4 to 6.*

MEATBALLS FLORENTINE

1 large onion, finely
    minced
1 stalk celery, finely
    minced
2 carrots, finely minced
3 tablespoons butter
1 teaspoon flour
1 cup hot beef bouillon
    or stock
salt and pepper to taste

½ lb. ground lean veal
1 lb. ground lean pork
    or ham
a pinch each of thyme and
    nutmeg
1 tablespoon minced
    parsley
1 clove garlic, grated
2 eggs, slightly beaten

*These delicious meatballs will make you wonder which came
first, the Swedish or the Florentine. Serve these as an entrée
or as an hors d'oeuvre.*

Sauté onion, celery and carrots in butter until they begin to
brown, sprinkle with flour and stirring constantly cook until
flour begins to brown. Add bouillon and season to taste. Set
aside and keep hot. Combine veal and pork, adding rest of ingredients, seasoning to taste. Mix and blend well and shape
mixture into small balls the size of walnuts; roll in seasoned
flour. Place meatballs in vegetable mixture, cover pan and simmer very gently for about 1 hour. Serve in a deep dish with
the vegetable sauce and sprinkle with a little lemon juice. Can
be served sprinkled with Parmesan cheese. Makes about 24
balls. *Serves 4 to 6.*

ORIENTAL MEAT PIE

1 lb. chopped beef
⅛ lb. prosciutto or ham,
    minced
2 slices bread, soaked
    and squeezed dry
salt and pepper
2 egg yolks
2 tablespoons grated
    Parmesan cheese
1 teaspoon butter
2 tablespoons olive oil
1 teaspoon rosemary,
    chopped fine

1 clove garlic chopped
    fine (optional)

SAUCE

½ can tomato paste
    dissolved in 1 cup
    warm water
1 teaspoon butter
1 tablespoon olive oil
salt and pepper

*A delicious meat loaf, shaped into a giant hamburger, and
spiced with rosemary . . . called "Galetta."*

With your hands, mix and blend together beef, prosciutto and bread. Add salt and pepper, egg yolks, grated cheese and butter. Mix well, working it as you would dough. Mold into a large ball, then flatten into the form of a large hamburger about 1 inch thick. Butter a round baking dish or pan, and place the meat pie in it. Mix rosemary and garlic in the 2 tablespoons of olive oil and spread over meat. Bake in moderate oven (about 350° F.) until meat is cooked and has acquired a golden-colored crust. Meanwhile prepare sauce: heat olive oil and butter in a saucepan, add tomato paste dissolved in warm water, and cook for a few minutes, or until it thickens. When meat is done, remove from pan, place on serving dish, pour over it whatever oil is in pan, and spread sauce over all. Serve hot. *Serves 4.*

OMELET STUFFED BEEF ROLL

1 large slice bottom
round of beef, ¼"
thick (about 1 lb.)
1 tablespoon flour
2 tablespoons milk
1 egg, beaten
pinch of salt
1 tablespoon grated
Parmesan cheese
3 tablespoons olive oil
3 or 4 tablespoons
chopped parsley

5 or 6 slices prosciutto
or ham
⅛ lb. salt pork, chopped
fine
4 tablespoons butter
1 medium onion,
chopped
½ cup water
rice or macaroni

Have slice of beef butterflied and pounded thin. Flank steak may be used, split lengthwise with grain, almost in two; open and pound uncut edge flat; steak is now half as thick and twice as wide. Combine and blend flour and milk well together, add the egg, salt and cheese; mix well. Heat 2 tablespoons olive oil in a frying pan about the size of the slice of meat, turn the egg mixture into it. As it cooks, draw edges toward center

67

with a knife until whole is set, forming a very thin, flat omelet. Arrange the omelet on top of the slice of beef and cover completely with chopped parsley. Top with slices of prosciutto, roll and tie firmly to hold together. Place beef roll in a casserole with the remaining olive oil, the butter, salt pork and onion. Season with salt and pepper and cover tightly. Cook over low heat, turning often so as to brown evenly on all sides. When well-browned, add ½ cup water, cover, and continue cooking for 1 hour over low heat, adding a little more water if necessary. Remove string, slice and serve with rice or macaroni seasoned with the pan gravy. It makes very attractive slices. *Serves 4.*

POT ROAST IN BURGUNDY

3 lbs. beef roast (round, chuck or rump)	3 tablespoons olive oil
1 or 2 slices fat salt pork	½ cup dried mushrooms
⅛ teaspoon each pepper and allspice	1 cup broth, stock or bouillon
2 cloves	2 tablespoons tomato paste, dissolved in 1 cup water
1 cup chopped onion	
1 cup chopped carrots	1 clove garlic, crushed
1 cup chopped celery	¼ cup cognac
2 to 3 cups Burgundy	1 teaspoon butter
3 tablespoons butter	

From the border of France and Italy (Piedmont) comes this aromatic pot roast, seasoned with red wine and cognac.

Cut deep gashes in beef. Slice salt pork very thin, rub with pepper and allspice and place in the gashes in meat. Tie meat so as to keep its shape. Place meat in a deep dish, add the cloves and ½ cup each of chopped onion, carrot and celery. Pour the wine over all and let meat stand in this marinade for 12 to 24 hours, turning frequently. Lift meat from marinade and blot dry. Strain marinade and set aside. Brown meat in a pan with 3 tablespoons of butter and the olive oil and the remaining chopped onion, carrot and celery, turning often until well browned. Add the marinade, cover and let cook, turning occasionally until marinade has completely evaporated. Soak mushrooms in a little warm water until soft; drain and chop. When marinade has evaporated, moisten meat with the broth and add the mushrooms, seasoning lightly with salt and pepper; cover and let cook over a low heat for about 2½ hours. When done, lift meat from pan (keep warm), add to contents of pan the dissolved tomato paste, the garlic and the cognac. Blend and let cook over high heat for a few minutes, remove garlic and add a teaspoon of butter; taste for seasoning and pour into gravy boat. Slice meat and top each slice with a little sauce and serve with pan-browned little white onions. *Serves 6.*

SAUERBRATEN

3 to 4 lbs. cross rib of beef or bottom round	3 bay leaves
salt and pepper	1 teaspoon peppercorns
garlic (optional)	½ cup sugar
2 cups vinegar or sauterne	3 tablespoons olive oil or fat
2 cups water	¼ cup raisins
½ cup sliced onion	4 to 6 gingersnaps
	1 cup thick sour cream

Sauerbraten is a German pot roast which is first marinated for several days, imparting to it a distinctive flavor.

Rub meat with cut surface of garlic and salt and pepper. Place in a deep earthenware dish or bowl. Heat vinegar, water, onion, bay leaves, peppercorns and ¼ cup sugar together, but do not boil. Pour hot mixture over meat, cover bowl and refrigerate from 4 to 8 days, turning meat each day. Drain, reserving marinade. Brown meat in hot olive oil, add half the marinade, cover pan and simmer until tender, 2 to 3 hours, adding more marinade as required to keep liquid about ½" deep in pan. Remove meat, slice for serving and keep hot. Strain pan sauce; skim off fat. Melt remaining ¼ cup sugar in a skillet, add strained liquid gradually, then raisins and gingersnaps. Cook until thickened and smooth; stir in sour cream and when hot pour over meat. Gravy may be served "straight" without adding sugar, raisins and gingersnaps. In that case, thicken the gravy with a little flour and stir in the sour cream. *Serves 6 to 8.*

STEAK SURPRISES

1 tablespoon butter
1 tablespoon tomato
   paste
salt and pepper
½ cup water or stock
⅓ cup sherry
½ tablespoon chopped
   parsley
4 slices tenderloin of
   beef, cut ½" thick
4 thin slices prosciutto or
   ham

4 slices mozzarella
   cheese, sliced thin
½ cup flour
1 egg, well beaten
1 teaspoon grated
   Parmesan cheese
1 cup bread crumbs
2 tablespoons butter
1 tablespoon olive oil
1 lb. sliced mushrooms
   sautéed in butter

First, prepare sauce. Melt 1 tablespoon of butter in saucepan, add tablespoon of tomato paste, salt and pepper. Mix and blend thoroughly. Add ½ cup stock or water and cook for a few minutes. Add ⅓ cup sherry, mix thoroughly and let simmer slowly until sauce thickens. Just before removing from heat, add chopped parsley. While sauce is cooking, prepare meat. Slit each slice of beef as you would a bun, leaving one end closed. Sprinkle opening lightly with salt and pepper, then place a slice of prosciutto in the slit, top with a slice of mozzarella, press slices of beef together. Roll first in flour, dip in beaten egg to which has been added a teaspoon of grated cheese, then roll in bread crumbs. Fry gently in butter and olive oil until golden-brown on both sides (about 4 to 5 minutes on each side). Arrange Steak Surprises around edges of a round serving dish, in center of which heap sautéed mushrooms. Cover each steak with sauce or serve sauce separately. *Serves 4.* (Club steaks, boned and trimmed, may be substituted for tenderloin.)

BEEF STEW WITH FENNEL

2 lbs. boneless beef for stew, cut into small cubes	½ cup Chablis or Burgundy
2 slices prosciutto, or bacon, chopped	½ tablespoon flour
	2 tablespoons tomato paste
1 stalk celery, chopped	warm water
1 small onion, chopped	1 clove garlic, minced
1 tablespoon olive oil	1 tablespoon chopped parsley
1 teaspoon butter	
salt and pepper	½ teaspoon fennel seeds

Place chopped prosciutto, celery and onion in a skillet with olive oil and butter, and brown. As soon as vegetables begin to color slightly, add the meat; brown meat and vegetables thoroughly. Season with salt and pepper and pour wine over all. Mix and let wine evaporate slightly. Sprinkle flour over meat; mix, then stir in tomato paste. Let cook 2 or 3 minutes, then add warm water sufficient to cover meat. Cover pan, lower heat and simmer until meat is tender and pan sauce thickened. Mix the garlic, parsley and fennel seeds together and add to the stew; mix well and let cook for another few minutes to absorb the flavoring, and serve. *Serves 4.*

BEEF STEW IN RED WINE

3 lbs. lean beef for stew,
   cut into large cubes
1 onion, chopped
2 cloves garlic, chopped
2 tablespoons olive oil
1 tablespoon tomato
   paste, dissolved in 1
   cup water

MARINADE

¼ teaspoon nutmeg
¼ teaspoon thyme
2 bay leaves
1 clove garlic, sliced
2 cups Burgundy (or
   any dry red wine)
¼ teaspoon salt
⅛ teaspoon pepper

Combine ingredients for marinade in a bowl, add the meat and marinate overnight, or at least 4 or 5 hours before cooking. When ready to cook, lift meat cubes from marinade and set aside. Strain marinade and reserve 1 cup. In a deep skillet brown the onion and garlic in olive oil until lightly colored, add meat and let it brown gently. Moisten with the marinade liquid about ¼ cup at a time and let evaporate after each addition. Add dissolved tomato paste, cover and cook gently over a moderate heat for about 40 to 45 minutes, or until meat is tender to the fork. *Serves 4 to 6.*

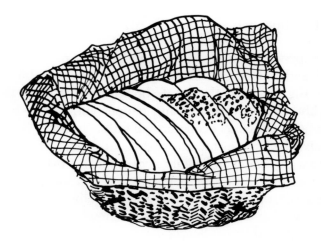

STUFFED BEEF ROLLS, NEAPOLITAN (Braciole)

¼ lb. chopped beef
1 tablespoon grated
 Parmesan cheese
2 tablespoons raisins
1 clove garlic, minced or
 ¼ teaspoon garlic
 powder
1 tablespoon chopped
 parsley
salt and pepper to taste
1 egg, slightly beaten
4 thin slices of top or
 bottom round of beef,
 4″ x 6″

4 thin slices prosciutto,
 salami or ham
¼ cup olive oil
1 small onion, chopped
 fine
1 clove garlic, crushed
¼ cup dry white wine
1 16-oz. can tomatoes,
 cut up
salt and pepper to taste

"Braciole" makes a delicious entrée, served with a vegetable and/or salad. The sauce is perfect for pasta or rice.

Combine first six ingredients, mixing thoroughly and adding enough beaten egg to hold together. Pound meat slices thin; place a slice of prosciutto on each slice of beef and spread a portion of the beef mixture on each slice (a sliver of salt pork may be added if desired). Roll each slice and secure with toothpicks. Brown beef rolls in hot olive oil, with onion and garlic; remove garlic when it begins to color. Add wine a little at a time and allow to evaporate; add tomatoes and juice, season with salt and pepper; lower heat, cover, and simmer gently for 1½ hours or until beef rolls are tender. Serve beef rolls covered with sauce. *Serves 4.*

STUFFED BEEF ROLL, SICILIAN

1 large thick slice top
  round of beef, about
  1 lb.
¼ cup olive oil
1 onion, minced
½ cup Burgundy
1 can tomato paste,
  dissolved in 1 cup
  warm water
2 cups warm water
2 lbs. fresh peas, shelled,
  or 1 can peas,
  drained

FILLING

½ lb. chopped beef,
  bottom round or
  chuck

4 slices bread, soak in
  water and squeezed
  dry
pinch of nutmeg
3 eggs, slightly beaten
3 tablespoons grated
  Parmesan cheese
2 tablespoons chopped
  parsley
¼ teaspoon pepper
4 hard-cooked eggs,
  sliced
4 slices Italian salami,
  cut in slivers
⅛ lb. fresh provolone
  cheese, cut in slivers

Prepare Filling: Mix chopped beef and bread in a bowl, add slightly-beaten eggs, grated cheese, nutmeg, parsley and pepper. Mix thoroughly until well blended.

Have the slice of beef butterflied in a roughly rectangular shape and pounded thin by butcher. The narrow width will form the base of the roll. Spread the meat with the chopped mixture, slightly wetting your hands to facilitate spreading it

on the meat evenly. Arrange the sliced hard-cooked eggs, slivers of salami and provolone cheese in alternate rows parallel to the narrowest width. Roll meat to resemble a thick salami. Tie firmly and brown in olive oil with onion. When onion is a golden color, add wine; season with salt and pepper and continue browning for a few minutes longer. Add dissolved tomato paste and the water. Cover and simmer for about 1 hour, or until meat is tender. During the last 10 or 15 minutes of cooking time add shelled peas and cook along with meat until peas are tender. If canned peas are used, drain and add during the last 5 minutes of cooking time. To serve: lift meat from pan, remove string, slice and cover with peas and sauce. *Serves 4.*

SURPRISE ROAST ROLL OF BEEF

1 large thin slice bottom round beef, ¼″ thick, about 1 lb.	¼ lb. salami
	1 egg
	salt and pepper
1 large thin slice veal, ¼″ thick, about ¾ lb.	1 clove garlic
	1 teaspoon butter
⅛ lb. lean salt pork	1 teaspoon rosemary

Have butcher butterfly a ½″ thick slice of bottom round and pound it thin. Have the same done with a slice of veal from the leg. In a chopping bowl mince salt pork and salami together. Add the egg, mix and blend well. Spread half of this mixture evenly on the slice of beef, then place the slice of veal on top and spread the balance of mixture on the slice of veal. Roll and tie securely so as to resemble a thick salami. Rub roll with clove of garlic, then butter and sprinkle with salt and pepper. Place in baking pan, sprinkle with rosemary and place in preheated 350° F. oven for 1½ to 2 hours or until meat is tender and nicely browned, turning often. Remove string, slice and serve with vegetables and potatoes. *Serves 4.*

BEEF TENDERLOIN IN PASTRY

3½ to 4 lb. piece sirloin tip (silver tip) or fillet of beef

thin slices of prosciutto or ham

1 or 2 small cans of pâté de foie gras, or liver pâté

½ cup beef stock or bouillon

melted butter

chopped black truffles (optional)

pastry for 2-crust pie

1 egg, beaten

The French call this "Filet en Chemise," the Italians "Filetto in Camicia"—all very dressed up. It is well worth the work involved and your guests will be deliciously impressed.

Have meat trimmed of all fat. Wipe the meat with a cloth dipped in brandy. Slice meat into 6 or 8 equal parts without separating the slices. Spread a little pâté on each slice and place a thin slice of prosciutto on each. Reshape the meat, tie if necessary, and roast in a preheated 375° F. oven for about 10 to 15 minutes, or until half done, basting often with the stock. Remove from oven, brush with melted butter and cool slightly. Spread the remaining pâté thinly over the meat and sprinkle with chopped truffles. Roll out pastry into a thin sheet and wrap the meat in it, securing it neatly. Brush with beaten egg and bake on a baking sheet in a hot 400° F. oven for about 15 to 25 minutes, or until crust is nicely browned. Serve with a mushroom sauce made as follows: slice ½ lb. fresh mushrooms (or use sliced, canned mushrooms) and sauté in about 3 tablespoons butter; season with salt and pepper. Add 1 small shallot, or clove of garlic, finely chopped, ⅓ cup stock or bouillon mixed with ½ tablespoon flour and ⅓ cup Madeira or dry sherry. Bring to a boil and simmer slowly for a few minutes. Add a little chopped parsley and serve. *Serves 6 to 8.*

TRIPE, FLORENTINE

2 lbs. honeycomb tripe
1 onion studded with 5 cloves
½ teaspoon salt
¼ cup olive oil
1 onion, chopped
3 cloves garlic, chopped fine
2 tablespoons chopped parsley
3 or 4 stalks celery, cut into ½" pieces

3 carrots, sliced
1 16-oz. can tomatoes, cut up
2 teaspoons dry basil
½ teaspoon rosemary, crumbled
3 tablespoons butter
2 tablespoon grated Parmesan cheese

Wash tripe several times. Cut into very thin strips or little squares; cover with cold water, add salt and whole onion. Bring to a boil, lower heat and simmer for 1 hour. Drain thoroughly. In a heavy saucepan or Dutch oven sauté onion, garlic and parsley in hot olive oil for about 1 minute, stirring constantly. Add the vegetables and continue sautéing until vegetables are lightly colored, about 10 minutes. Add the drained tripe, tomatoes and juice from can, salt and pepper to taste, and the basil and rosemary; mix and blend well. Cover and simmer gently for about 2 hours, stirring often to keep tripe from scorching or sticking to bottom of pan. This recipe does not call for any additional liquid. However, should the ingredients become too dry, add a little broth or bouillon. When done, stir in the butter and grated cheese, and serve. *Serves 4.*

TRIPE ALLA ROMANA

2 lbs. honeycomb tripe
1 onion studded with 5
  cloves
½ teaspoon salt
1 tablespoon olive oil
2 tablespoons butter
1 small onion, minced
1 medium carrot, minced
1 stalk celery, minced
2 slices prosciutto or
  ham, minced

⅓ cup sauterne
1 16-oz. can tomatoes,
  strained
2 tablespoons tomato
  paste, dissolved in a
  little bouillon, stock
  or water
salt and pepper to taste
grated Parmesan cheese
chopped mint leaves
  (optional)

Wash tripe several times. Cut into very thin strips or little squares; cover with cold water, add salt and the whole onion studded with cloves. Bring to a boil, lower heat and simmer for 1 hour. Drain thoroughly. In a heavy saucepan or Dutch oven sauté the chopped vegetables in hot olive oil and butter until they are softened. Add the prosciutto and tripe and gently sauté with the vegetables, stirring constantly for about 5 minutes, adding wine a little at a time and allowing wine to evaporate after each addition. Add strained tomatoes, dissolved tomato paste, salt and pepper to taste. Cover and simmer for 1 to 1½ hours, or until tripe is very tender to the fork and the sauce has thickened. Add a touch of mint leaves and serve sprinkled with Parmesan cheese. *Serves 4.*

Lamb

BRAISED LAMB, EASTER STYLE

1 small leg of lamb
1 tablespoon butter
2 tablespoons olive oil
1 large onion, sliced
1 large carrot, diced
2 stalks celery, diced

2 teaspoons chopped parsley
1 teaspoon salt
½ teaspoon pepper
1 cup dry white wine
1 cup water or bouillon

From Italy, where lamb is traditional at Easter, comes this easy and excellent top-of-the-stove method for "roasting" lamb.

Melt butter and oil in large heavy pan or Dutch oven, and brown leg of lamb slowly but thoroughly on all sides. When browned, lift from pan, set aside and keep warm. Place onion, carrot, celery and parsley in pan and, lowering flame, sauté until well browned and soft; return meat to pan and pour over it juice drained from it while standing. Add salt and pepper. Raise heat and pour wine over lamb gradually, ⅓ cup at a time, letting each measure of wine evaporate thoroughly before adding the next. When all the wine has evaporated, cover pan and, lowering the flame, moisten lamb with water, ½ cup at a time, replacing cover each time. Let lamb cook slowly until tender (2 to 3 hours, depending upon size of leg), turning meat often during cooking period. Remove meat to serving dish. The pan sauce should be rather thick. Skim fat off and strain. Pour into gravy boat and serve with lamb. *Serves 6.*

LAMB CACCIATORA, ROMAN STYLE

1½ lbs. lean tender
boneless lamb, cut
in cubes
2 tablespoons olive oil
½ teaspoon salt
¼ teaspoon pepper
1 clove garlic, minced
1 teaspoon rosemary,
crumbled

½ teaspoon dry sage
leaves, crushed
½ tablespoon flour
½ cup wine vinegar,
diluted with ½ cup
water
3 anchovy fillets

This is a favorite dish of the Roman kitchen. The lamb should be young, tender and preferably a piece from the leg, lean and cut into pieces a bit larger than for stew.

Place lamb in a frying pan with olive oil. Brown pieces thoroughly over a high flame, add salt and pepper, stirring constantly, so that each piece acquires an even brown coating. When well browned, add the garlic, rosemary, and sage. Continue browning a little longer, then sprinkle with the flour and blend. Stir in diluted vinegar and mix everything well, scraping bottom and sides of pan. Lower heat, cover and let cook for about 15 to 20 minutes or until meat is tender. If sauce becomes too dry while cooking, add a little water from time to time. In the meantime, in a little bowl make a paste of the anchovy fillets, crushing and dissolving them in a tablespoon of the pan sauce. When the meat is cooked, add anchovy paste to the meat, mix well and cook for another minute. Arrange on serving dish with pan sauce, which should be rather thick, dark, and not too abundant. *Serves 4.*

LAMB CHOPS IN PASTRY

6 rib lamb chops,
  Frenched (bone
  exposed)
2 tablespoons butter
¼ cup Marsala or sherry
salt and pepper to taste
¼ cup dried mushrooms
⅛ lb. prosciutto or ham,
  minced
⅛ lb. pickled tongue,
  minced (optional)
2 tablespoons grated
  Parmesan cheese

plain pastry for 2-crust pie
1 egg, slightly beaten

SAUCE

3 tablespoons butter
2 tablespoons flour
1 cup hot milk
salt and pepper
pinch of nutmeg
1 egg yolk, slightly
  beaten

Soak mushrooms in 1 cup warm water for 15 minutes, drain and mince. Brown chops in hot butter on both sides. Moisten with Marsala and raise heat to let evaporate. Season chops with salt and pepper. Lift chops from pan and cool. Mean-

81

while, prepare sauce: melt and heat butter in a saucepan, stir in flour. Add hot milk all at once, stirring constantly. Season with salt, pepper and nutmeg and, stirring constantly, continue cooking until sauce starts to thicken. Remove from heat, add egg yolk, mix well; return to heat and cook 1 minute longer. Remove from heat, add mushrooms, prosciutto, tongue and grated cheese, mixing and blending all ingredients thoroughly. Holding each chop by the bared bone, dip into the sauce, one at a time, coating meat thickly; set chops aside to cool. Prepare your favorite pie pastry or use prepared pastry mix. Roll out pastry about ¼" thick; cut into rounds double the size of each chop. Place a chop on lower half of a round, leaving bone exposed; fold over the other half, pinching edges together. Place chops on buttered baking pan or cookie sheet. Brush lightly with beaten egg and place in preheated hot 400° F. oven for about 15 minutes. Arrange in a ring on a round warm serving dish, placing paper frills on exposed bones. Fill center with fried potatoes. *Serves 3.*

LAMB CHOPS IN WINE

6 rib, loin or shoulder
    lamb chops
1 large clove garlic
salt and pepper
2 tablespoons butter
2 tablespoons olive oil

6 or 8 scallions, chopped
1 tablespoon chopped
    parsley
2 tablespoons flour
1½ cups dry white wine

Rub chops with garlic, salt and pepper. Combine and heat butter and olive oil in large skillet. Brown chops on both sides in hot butter and olive oil mixture. As chops are browned, remove to a baking dish. Add a teaspoon of butter to pan where chops were browned and sauté scallions and parsley until scallions are soft. Stir in flour, blending well; gradually add the wine and, stirring constantly, cook until it starts to thicken. Pour over the lamb chops, cover pan and bake in preheated moderate 350° F. oven for about 20 to 25 minutes. Remove cover and continue cooking for 10 minutes longer. Serve hot with potatoes or vegetables and a salad. *Serves 3.*

DICED LAMB AND PEAS WITH WHITE WINE

1½ lbs. lamb for stew (lean), cut into small pieces	¼ teaspoon pepper
	1 clove garlic, crushed
	½ teaspoon rosemary
2 tablespoons olive oil	½ cup dry white wine
½ teaspoon salt	1 can peas, drained

A simple, savory one-pan dish—just serve with a tossed salad.

Place lamb in large frying pan, or skillet, with olive oil. Brown well on all sides over high flame. Add salt, pepper, garlic and rosemary. Continue browning a little longer. Add wine, mix everything well together, scraping bottom of pan. Lower flame and cook slowly about 40 minutes, or until meat is tender, then add peas. Mix peas gently with meat. Cover and simmer for about 5 minutes, and then serve. *Serves 4.*

LEG OF LAMB SAUERBRATEN

1 small leg of lamb	2 bay leaves
salt and pepper	1 tablespoon pickling spices
garlic (optional)	
2 cups vinegar or sauterne	1 teaspoon peppercorns
	¼ cup sugar
2 cups water	2 tablespoons olive oil
1 medium onion, sliced	¼ cup raisins (optional)

Rub meat with cut surface of garlic and with salt and pepper. Place in a deep dish or bowl. Heat vinegar, water, onion, bay leaves, spices, peppercorns and sugar together; do not boil. Pour hot mixture over meat, cover bowl and refrigerate 1 to 4 days, turning meat in marinade night and morning. Drain saving marinade. Brown meat in hot olive oil, add half the strained marinade, cover pan and simmer until tender, 2 to 3 hours, adding more strained marinade as required to keep liquid about ½" deep in pan. When done, remove meat, slice for serving and keep hot. Add raisins to pan liquid and thicken for gravy by adding 1 tablespoon of flour mixed with a little water. *Serves 6.*

STUFFED LEG OF LAMB, RENAISSANCE

5 or 6 lb. leg of lamb	5 or 6 chicken livers,
1 clove garlic	cut up
salt and pepper	½ teaspoon mint leaves
¼ cup olive oil	1 lb. potatoes, cut into
¼ cup butter	little rounds or cubes
1½ cups Chablis	1 lb. small white onions
½ lb. Italian sausage,	
sweet	

We must thank the Florentines for this superb roast, which is a delight to the senses.

Have butcher remove bone from the leg of lamb. Wipe with a damp cloth. Remove casing from sausage and crumble meat. Sauté sausage meat lightly in a little butter, add chicken livers and continue sautéing until livers are tender. Blend in mint; stuff lamb cavity with this mixture. Sew or skewer opening. Rub leg with garlic or insert slivers of garlic into meat here and there. Rub leg with salt and pepper. Place olive oil, butter and lamb in a roasting pan and sear in a hot 450° F. oven

on all sides until well browned. Moisten with wine, reduce
temperature to 350° F. and roast, figuring on 20 minutes per lb.
Baste frequently with liquid in pan. One hour before lamb is
done, add potatoes and onions to pan and continue cooking
until meat and vegetables are done. Arrange leg of lamb on a
heated serving dish, surrounded by the potatoes and onions,
and serve with the rich gravy from the pan. *Serves 6.*

ROAST SHOULDER LAMB, RENAISSANCE

1 rolled, boned shoulder of lamb, tied for roasting	½ cup sauterne
	1 small can liver pâté or pâté de foie gras
1 carrot, minced	2 tablespoons cognac
1 onion, minced	1 tablespoon butter
1 stalk celery, minced	2 tablespoons flour
1 teaspoon dried mint leaves	milk
	pinch of nutmeg
1 tablespoon butter	1 small truffle, sliced
1 tablespoon olive oil	(optional)

Florentine culinary art at its best—a majestic offering.

Place meat in roasting pan over vegetables, butter and olive
oil, with mint leaves; sear thoroughly on all sides on top of
stove, seasoning with salt and pepper. Then roast in preheated
350° F. oven for about 2 hours, moistening with wine and bast-

ing often. When done, lift meat from pan and place on oven-proof serving dish. Remove string and carefully slice meat roll, keeping its shape; spread on each slice a little of the liver pâté. Tie roll again lengthwise to retain shape, or pass a long skewer through center lengthwise. *Prepare sauce*: strain pan juices, add the cognac and enough milk to make 1½ cups liquid. Melt butter in saucepan, stir in flour, then milk mixture and, stirring constantly, let thicken. Blend in truffle, add dash of nutmeg; taste for seasoning and spread thickened sauce over meat. Return to oven for about 15 minutes. Serve immediately. *Serves 6.*

ROLLED STUFFED SHOULDER LAMB

1 shoulder of lamb, boned	salt and pepper
	1 large onion
1 lb. sweet Italian sausages, casing removed	1 carrot
	pinch of thyme
	1 bay leaf
1 finely chopped onion	1 clove garlic (optional)
1 tablespoon chopped parsley	3 tablespoons melted butter
1 egg	1 cup beef bouillon
1 cup bread crumbs	

Pound shoulder of lamb to flatten out well. Mix next 6 ingredients well, seasoning with salt and pepper to taste. Spread this stuffing on the lamb. Roll up and tie with string. Place in a roasting pan with onion, carrot, thyme, bay leaf and garlic. Pour over melted butter and bake in a hot 400° F. oven for 20 minutes, basting and turning often to brown all sides. Add bouillon, lower temperature to 350° F. and continue cooking for about 2 hours. When done, lift meat from pan onto a warm serving platter. Remove vegetables from pan, skim off the fat and make a gravy by adding 1 tablespoon of flour mixed with a little water. Slice meat and serve hot with the gravy. *Serves 6.*

LAMB STEW WITH ARTICHOKES

1½ to 2 lbs. boneless
    lamb, cut into cubes
    for stew
flour
2 thin slices salt pork,
    chopped
1 tablespoon butter
1 tablespoon olive oil

1 teaspoon leaf sage
1 cup Chablis
4 small fresh artichokes
    or 2 packages frozen
    artichokes
2 tablespoons chopped
    parsley
juice of 2 lemons

Lightly brown salt pork in butter and olive oil in a deep skillet. Dredge lamb pieces in a little flour and brown in same skillet, stirring constantly, and adding the sage. When well browned add the wine, a little at a time, letting it evaporate. Meanwhile prepare artichokes: remove stems and pull off rough outer leaves; cut off one-quarter of the tops. Cut into eighths and remove the choke. Wash them in cold water to which a little lemon juice has been added, and drain. Add the artichokes to lamb, cover and cook gently over moderate heat for about 1 hour and, if necessary, add a little water or stock now and then. About 5 minutes before lamb is ready to serve, stir in parsley and lemon juice. When done, serve lamb and artichokes on a warm platter and pour the pan sauce over all. (If frozen artichokes are used, thaw, drain and add to lamb about 15 or 20 minutes before it is done.) *Serves 4.*

LAMB STEW, WITH OLIVES, COUNTRY STYLE (POTTACHIO)

1½ to 2 lbs. boneless
    lean lamb, cut up in
    1½" pieces
2 tablespoons olive oil
2 cloves garlic, minced
2 teaspoons rosemary,
    crushed

½ cup sauterne
salt and pepper
1 tablespoon tomato
    paste, dissolved in ½
    cup warm water
1 can ripe olives, drained

This simple country dish from the Marches of Italy is a gourmet's delight.

Brown pieces of lamb in hot olive oil until thoroughly browned on all sides; add garlic and rosemary and continue browning until garlic darkens. Stir in wine and, stirring constantly, let evaporate. Season with salt and pepper to taste. Lower heat, add dissolved tomato paste, cover and continue cooking slowly until meat is tender, about 20 minutes. Add a little water, if needed, while cooking. Ten minutes before meat is done, add olives and cook with meat until heated through and olives have acquired the same glaze as meat. Serve hot with pan sauce over all. Sauce should not be thin nor too abundant. *Serves 4.*

Pork

BRAISED PORK IN PIQUANT SAUCE

3 to 4 lb. piece loin of
  pork
salt and pepper
slivers of salt pork
1 teaspoon rosemary
1 clove garlic, minced
4 slices prosciutto or ham
2 small onions, sliced
1 carrot, cut up
1 stalk celery, cut up
2 tablespoons butter
½ cup vinegar
1 cup broth or bouillon
2 tablespoons capers
2 small or 1 large hot
  pickled finger
  peppers, chopped

Have pork boned, rolled and tied to resemble a thick salami.
Make incisions in meat and fill with slivers of salt pork rolled
in rosemary and garlic. Arrange slices of prosciutto in bottom
of Dutch oven or deep casserole with onion, carrot, celery and
butter. Place meat on top and sear over high heat for about
12 to 15 minutes, turning often to brown evenly. Moisten with
broth and vinegar. Cover and let cook gently over moderate
heat until tender, figuring 40 to 45 minutes per pound. When
done, remove meat to warm serving dish. Strain contents of

pan, spooning off as much fat as possible, into a small sauce-pan. Add capers and peppers and cook for a few minutes, then strain again. Slice meat and pour sauce over all. *Serves 4 to 6.*

PORK CHOPS WITH HERBS

4 large pork chops
   (center cut)
1 to 2 teaspoons crushed,
   dried rosemary
1 teaspoon dried sage
   leaves
1 clove garlic, minced

dash of pepper
¼ teaspoon salt
water
1 tablespoon butter
¼ cup sauterne or
   Chablis

Combine herbs, garlic, salt and pepper. Rub mixture on both sides of chops and place chops in a skillet. Pour enough water into skillet to just cover chops. Cook, covered, over low heat for about 1 hour. When water has evaporated, add butter and brown chops on both sides. Add wine. Bring to boil and re-move from heat. Arrange chops in a warm serving dish and pour pan sauce over them. *Serves 4.*

PORK CHOPS, NEAPOLITAN STYLE

4 loin pork chops
2 sweet peppers, cut into
   1″ strips
½ lb. fresh mushrooms,
   sliced
3 tablespoons olive oil

1 clove garlic, whole and
   crushed
salt and pepper to taste
1 tablespoon tomato
   paste, dissolved in
   ½ cup warm water

Brown garlic in olive oil in a frying pan and when it starts to color, remove. Add chops to pan and brown slowly on both sides, seasoning with salt and pepper. Remove chops from pan and keep warm. Pour dissolved tomato paste into pan, add the peppers and mushrooms and sauté for about 10 minutes over a moderate heat, then add the chops. Cover pan and cook slowly until chops are well done. *Serves 2 to 4.*

ROAST STUFFED FRESH HAM

1 fresh ham
2 cups sauterne
parboiled sweet potatoes
    and onions

STUFFING

2 tablespoons olive oil
2 tablespoons chopped
    onion

2 cups soft bread cubes
3 cups chopped tart
    apples
½ cup chopped celery
wine
salt and paprika

Have the butcher bone the fresh ham for stuffing. Take fresh ham from refrigerator at least ½ hour before cooking. It may be rubbed well with a cut clove of garlic, fresh sage leaves or dried rosemary or thyme. If desired, dredge with flour. Prepare stuffing: sauté onion in olive oil until soft and transparent; combine with bread cubes, apples and celery. Moisten with a little wine and season with salt and paprika. Stuff ham and sew or skewer opening. Place fat side up in a pan in preheated 350° F. oven. Cook 30 to 45 minutes per lb., basting every half hour with wine. Add parboiled sweet potatoes (jackets removed) and onions during the last hour of roasting time. Serve ham surrounded by sweet potatoes and onions. Thicken the drippings with flour for gravy. A roast fresh ham is good served with sauerkraut and caraway seeds, or red cabbage.

ROAST LOIN OF PORK, ADRIATIC

4 to 5 lb. loin of pork,
    center cut
fennel or anise seeds
black pepper, coarsely
    ground
salt
2 or 3 cloves garlic,
    minced

3 large apples
juice of 1 or 2 lemons
¼ teaspoon cinnamon
2 teaspoons sugar
3 large potatoes, pared
    and cubed

Have fat trimmed off pork, bones cracked and backbone partially severed for easy carving. Rub salt well into meat, between ribs and severed backbone. Make a few incisions in meat and insert a generous amount of anise seeds and pepper into cuts and into cracks of bones. Place in open roasting pan, fat side up. Bake uncovered in moderate 350° F. oven 35 to 40 minutes per pound. Pork must be well-cooked. Core apples, do not pare, cut into ½" thick rounds and dip in lemon juice to which has been added cinnamon and sugar. Parboil potatoes for 8 minutes and drain. One hour before meat is done, drain a little of the fat from pan; arrange potatoes sprinkled with pepper and salt at one end of pan; apple slices at other. Continue roasting until meat is tender and potatoes and apples browned, turning potatoes and apples occasionally to brown evenly. Serve pork surrounded with potatoes and apples. Use rich, brown drippings in pan to make a gravy. *Serves 4 to 6.*

ROAST LOIN OF PORK IN RED WINE

4 to 5 lb. loin of pork,
    center cut
1 clove garlic, chopped
1 teaspoon rosemary

2 cups red wine, either a
    Burgundy or Chianti
2 tablespoons parsley

Have fat trimmed off pork, the bones cracked and the backbone partially severed for easy carving. Make a few incisions in meat. Mix garlic and rosemary together and insert into cuts and between cracked bones. Rub meat with salt and pepper and place in a deep pan, fat side up. Roast, uncovered, in a hot 400° F. oven for 30 minutes or until meat is nicely browned. Add wine and parsley to pan. Cover, reduce heat to moderate 350° F. and continue baking for another 2 to 2½ hours, or until tender. Remove cover for the last 15 or 20 minutes of cooking so as to reduce wine to half its amount. Serve with pan wine sauce poured over servings of meat, or serve it separately for individual helpings. *Serves 4 to 6.*

SAUSAGES AND MUSHROOMS WITH POLENTA

2 lbs. Italian sausages
  (hot or sweet)
2 tablespoons olive oil
2 cloves garlic, minced
1 teaspoon sage
1 16-oz. can tomatoes,
  strained

1 lb. mushrooms, cleaned
  and cut in quarters
salt and pepper
polenta (see page 201)

From the foot of the Italian Alps comes this peasant dish!

Cut sausages in half and brown in olive oil. Add garlic and sage and continue browning until garlic begins to color. Drain most of fat from pan. Add strained tomatoes and mushrooms; season with salt and pepper and let simmer for about 30 minutes or until sausages and mushrooms are tender and sauce is thickened a bit. Meanwhile prepare polenta; spread polenta on a warm serving dish and top with sausage and mushroom mixture. *Serves 4.*

SAUSAGES AND PEPPERS

8 Italian sausages
¼ cup boiling water
1 tablespoon olive oil
2 tablespoons tomato
    paste
1 clove garlic, whole

½ cup warm water
4 large sweet peppers,
    cleaned and sliced
    lengthwise
salt and pepper

Place sausage in large, deep frying pan with ¼ cup boiling water, cover and cook a few minutes until water evaporates, turning often. Uncover and pan brown for about 10 minutes until brown all over. Remove sausages to warm covered dish. Add olive oil and garlic to pan drippings and brown garlic lightly. Remove garlic, add peppers and sauté for a few minutes until softened. Add tomato paste dissolved in ½ cup warm water, mix and blend with peppers, cooking a few minutes longer. Return sausages to pan, cover and continue cooking peppers and sausages together until both are done. Serve hot. Figure on 2 sausages per serving. *Serves 4.*

SAVORY PORK STEW

1½ to 2 lbs. boneless
    fresh shoulder pork
    butt, cut into 1½"
    cubes
3 tablespoons olive oil
2 tablespoons butter
1 stalk celery, chopped
1 onion, chopped
⅓ cup white vinegar
3 carrots, sliced in
    rounds

2 cups water
1 tablespoon tomato
    paste
1 bay leaf
salt and pepper to taste
3 or 4 potatoes, pared
    and cut into quarters
    or eighths

The Italians love this delicious stew served with "polenta."

Have butcher cut butt into 1½" cubes, or you can easily do this yourself. Sauté celery and onion in olive oil and butter until softened and golden in color. Add meat and brown, turning often to prevent scorching. Moisten with vinegar, a little at a time, while meat is browning, and let vinegar evaporate. Add carrots, tomato paste dissolved in 2 cups of water, and bay leaf, and season to taste. Cover and let simmer for about 3 hours. One hour before it is done, add the potatoes. Serve with corn meal mush or polenta. (See page 201.) *Serves 4.*

Veal

VEAL "BIRDS," CACCIATORA (HUNTER STYLE)

1 to 1½ lbs. veal cutlet, sliced thin (Italian style), cut into 8 pieces about 4" or 5" square
6 or 8 chicken livers
1 tablespoon butter
2 slices prosciutto or lean bacon, or 2 slices salami
1 tablespoon sherry
1 teaspoon chopped parsley
3 or 4 sage leaves
salt and pepper to taste
8 narrow, thin slices lean salt pork or bacon
2 tablespoons butter
1 teaspoon flour
1 cup sherry
8 triangles of bread, toasted

Sauté chicken livers in 1 tablespoon butter, and chop fine with prosciutto, parsley and sage, and salt and pepper to taste. Add 1 tablespoon sherry; mix thoroughly. Flatten veal cutlets with a mallet or ask butcher to do it. On each slice of veal, spread some of the liver and prosciutto mixture until all is used. Roll each slice and wrap a thin, narrow slice of salt pork around each veal roll. Fasten each roll with toothpicks, securing salt pork to rolls. Sauté veal rolls in 2 tablespoons butter until thoroughly cooked and lightly browned. Sprinkle 1 teaspoon flour over "birds," add all but ¼ cup of the cup of sherry, and cook until wine is nearly evaporated. Arrange toasted slices of bread on serving dish, remove "birds" from pan and place them on toasted triangles. Add the remaining sherry to pan juices, mix well, scraping bottom and sides, simmer for a few seconds and pour over veal "birds" and toast. *Serves 4.*

VEAL BIRDS AND CHICKEN LIVERS EN BROCHETTE

12 small, thin slices of veal cut in 4" squares	sage leaves
	butter
6 thin slices prosciutto, cut in half	salt and pepper
	6 skewers
12 chicken livers	

These are the famous Italian "Uccelletti Scappati"—"Birds on the Wing."

Place a slice of prosciutto on each slice of meat and roll each slice—but not too tightly. On each skewer place a little meat roll, then a leaf of sage, a chicken liver, another meat roll, leaf of sage, and chicken liver. Sprinkle very lightly with salt and sauté in hot butter in frying pan, over moderate heat (covered) for about ½ hour, turning gently. If pan sauce becomes too thick, thin with a little water now and then. Serve with buttered rice; pour pan sauce over all. *Serves 4 to 6.*

97

VEAL BIRDS WITH TOMATO SAUCE

1 to 1½ lb. veal cutlets
(Italian style), cut
into thin 4" or
5" squares
¼ lb. mozzarella cheese,
slivered
anchovy fillets
pepper
1 tablespoon butter

2 tablespoons olive oil
1 tablespoon tomato
paste, dissolved in
½ cup warm water,
broth or bouillon
salt and pepper
1 tablespoon chopped
parsley

On each slice of meat place a few slivers of mozzarella, one or two anchovy fillets, a little pepper; then roll the slices and fasten with toothpicks. Slowly brown veal rolls in hot butter and olive oil, until tender. Remove from pan and keep warm on serving plate. Make a sauce by adding the dissolved tomato paste to drippings in pan, scraping sides and bottom, and simmer for a few minutes to thicken. Stir in chopped parsley, and pour over veal rolls. Serve hot. *Serves 4.*

BRAISED VEAL WITH CARROTS

2½ to 3 lbs. boneless
veal, in one piece
¼ lb. butter
1 clove garlic, cut in
slivers

2 bunches carrots, cut in
long, thin slices
salt and pepper

An inexpensive cut of veal can be used for this flavorful pot roast.

Tie meat if necessary to hold together. Sprinkle with salt and pepper. Melt and heat butter in Dutch oven or casserole, add meat and garlic and brown meat well, slowly, on all sides. When garlic becomes brown, remove, and when meat is thoroughly browned, cover and cook slowly in its own juices. Long, slow cooking does the trick. Figure on about 25 to 30 minutes per pound. Thirty minutes before meat is done, add carrots and cook, covered, until meat and carrots are tender, stirring carrots and turning meat occasionally. To serve, slice meat and arrange in an attractive mound in center of warm platter and surround with carrots. *Serves 4 to 6.*

STUFFED BREAST OF VEAL

1 breast of veal, with a
    pocket cut into it
½ lb. ground veal
1 lb. sweet Italian
    sausages, casing
    removed
salt and pepper
pinch of nutmeg
½ cup sherry
2 carrots, minced
2 small onions, minced

1 stalk celery, minced
½ teaspoon sage
½ teaspoon basil
2 tablespoons butter
⅛ lb. salt pork, chopped
2 cloves
salt and pepper
1 cup Chablis or any dry
    white wine
1 cup bouillon

Combine ground veal, sausage, salt and pepper to taste, and nutmeg. Add sherry, and with the hands mix and blend into a smooth mixture. Fill pocket of breast of veal; sew or skewer opening. Place minced vegetables, sage, basil, butter and salt pork in a large roasting pan and brown lightly on top of stove. Place stuffed breast of veal on top of vegetable mixture, season with salt and pepper, add the cloves, white wine and bouillon, cover tightly and roast in a preheated 375° F. oven until tender, turning occasionally and basting with the pan sauce. Figure on 25 to 30 minutes per lb. When done remove and keep warm. Strain pan sauce and thicken with a little flour. Serve veal sliced with the gravy. This is good served cold, also. *Serves 6.*

VEAL CHOPS IN CASSEROLE

4 veal chops, ½" thick
2 tablespoons flour
½ teaspoon salt
¼ teaspoon pepper
1 tablespoon butter
1 tablespoon olive oil
1 clove garlic, crushed
2 medium-sized potatoes, sliced
2 tablespoons butter

2 tablespoons olive oil
1 lb. fresh mushrooms, cleaned, washed and sliced
¼ cup dry white wine
1 tablespoon chopped parsley
½ teaspoon chopped chives

Mix salt and pepper with flour. Have chops trimmed neatly by butcher or do it yourself. Dust chops in flour. Heat 1 tablespoon butter and 1 tablespoon olive oil in frying pan and brown chops thoroughly and slowly on both sides, browning clove of garlic with them. At same time sauté potatoes in another frying pan in 2 tablespoons butter and 2 tablespoons olive oil. Butter sides and bottom of casserole and pour a little oil on the bottom. Place mushrooms on bottom of casserole and sprinkle with salt and pepper; arrange chops over them. Pour wine into pan where chops were browned, scrape sides and bottom and cook over high heat for a few seconds; pour over chops and mushrooms. Top with potatoes. Sprinkle parsley and chives over all. Cover casserole and cook in hot oven (425° F.) for 20 minutes. When done, remove cover and invert on serving dish, or serve right from casserole. *Serves 4.*

VEAL CHOPS "OTHELLO"

4 veal chops, cut 1" thick
1 teaspoon butter
4 slices prosciutto or
    ham, cut very thin
1 teaspoon Marsala or
    sherry
4 thin slices truffle
    (optional)
8 small, very thin slices
    mozzarella cheese

1 or 2 eggs, slightly
    beaten
bread crumbs
3 tablespoons butter
1 tablespoon olive oil
salt and pepper
4 anchovy fillets, cut up
1 teaspoon butter

Trim chops, then with sharp knife, make an even slit in each chop from the edge almost to the bone in the middle-of-the-loin thickness, or have butcher do it for you. Brown prosciutto or ham in 1 teaspoon butter, very lightly. Sprinkle with Marsala and let evaporate. Lift slices from pan and place on work board. Place a slice of truffle in center of each slice of prosciutto and fold or wrap prosciutto over it. Open slit of chops, place a thin slice of cheese in slit, top with the prosciutto and cover with another slice of cheese. Close the slit and press firmly together or pound with a mallet, to press edges firmly together. Dip chops in flour, then in egg, and then in bread crumbs. Brown on each side in 3 tablespoons butter and 1 tablespoon olive oil and cook gently until golden brown and tender. Lift from pan and keep warm on serving dish. Add 1 teaspoon butter and the anchovies to pan drippings, mixing and blending thoroughly, and pour this sauce over chops. Garnish dish with watercress and thin slices of lemon. *Serves 4.*

VEAL CUTLET, PARMESAN

1 lb. veal cutlet (Italian
style), 4 or 5 slices,
¼" thick
flour
1 or 2 eggs, slightly
beaten
salt and pepper to taste
2 cups bread crumbs
4 tablespoons grated
Parmesan cheese

¼ cup olive oil
"Quick" tomato sauce (see
page 189)
½ lb. mozzarella cheese,
sliced not too thin
freshly ground black
pepper
dots of butter

Dip cutlets in flour, then in beaten egg to which has been added salt, pepper and a teaspoon of grated Parmesan cheese, then in bread crumbs, coating cutlets well. Fry cutlets in hot olive oil and arrange in a baking pan or in individual baking dishes. Spread tomato sauce over each, sprinkle with grated Parmesan cheese, and top each cutlet with slices of mozzarella cheese. Sprinkle a little pepper over mozzarella and dot with butter. Bake in a preheated 350° F. oven for about 10 to 15 minutes, or until cheese is melted. Serve hot. *Serves 4.*

VEAL FRICASSEE WITH MUSHROOMS

1½ to 2 lbs. veal from
shoulder or loin, cut
in cubes
¼ cup butter
1 onion, cut in thin slices
1 bay leaf
1 stalk celery, cut up
salt and pepper
¾ cup dry white wine

2 tablespoons flour
2 cups broth
½ cup milk
½ lb. fresh mushrooms,
cleaned and sliced
2 tablespoons butter
juice of half a lemon
2 egg yolks
½ cup cream

Place ¼ cup butter, onion, bay leaf, celery, and veal in a pan and brown, turning pieces often until meat has acquired a good color. Season with salt and pepper. Add wine gradually and let cook until wine has almost evaporated. Dust with flour and mix well. Add broth and milk, cover and let simmer gently over moderate heat for about 1 hour or until veal is tender, stirring occasionally so meat does not stick to bottom of pan. Meanwhile, wash, dry and slice mushrooms. Sauté gently for about 5 minutes in 2 tablespoons butter, sprinkling with lemon juice and seasoning with salt and pepper. When veal is cooked, lift pieces from pan with fork and keep warm in a bowl. Strain contents of pan into a small bowl. Beat egg yolks well and while beating add the cream and the strained sauce, blending ingredients well together. Return meat to pan, pour sauce mixture over meat, add the sautéed mushrooms, mix ingredients gently and let cook over moderate heat for another 5 minutes. Serve with Risotto (see page 147). *Serves 4 to 6.*

VEAL KIDNEYS, TRIFOLATI

4 veal kidneys
½ cup flour
2 tablespoons olive oil
1 clove garlic, whole
    and crushed
salt and pepper
4 anchovy fillets,
    chopped

¼ cup sauterne, or sweet
    white wine or
    Madeira
1 tablespoon chopped
    parsley
1 tablespoon lemon juice

Remove fat from kidneys and slice as thin as possible. Roll slices lightly in flour. Brown garlic in hot olive oil and when it begins to color, add kidneys, season with salt and pepper. Sauté briskly for about 15 minutes. Add wine and anchovies, and continue cooking for another minute or two. Remove from heat, add lemon juice and parsley. Toss and serve immediately with pan sauce. *Serves 4.* Lamb kidneys may also be used.

VEAL AND PEPPERS, NEAPOLITAN STYLE

1 lb. veal cutlet, sliced thin (Italian style) and cut into 3" or 4" pieces

4 large sweet green peppers

⅓ cup olive oil

1 clove garlic, whole, crushed

1 16-oz. can tomatoes, drained and chopped

½ teaspoon salt

¼ teaspoon pepper

4 or 5 green olives, pitted and cut up

pinch of oregano

Use a large deep skillet for this simple, homey one-pan savory meal.

Cut peppers in halves, remove stalks and seeds, slice, wash and drain. Heat olive oil. When hot, put in veal and brown quickly, first on one side, then on the other. Add sliced peppers and garlic. Sauté peppers with veal and garlic for about 3 minutes, mixing constantly. Add tomatoes, salt and pepper, and blend with veal and peppers. Cook all together slowly, uncovered, until meat and peppers are tender, about 15 to 20 minutes. Add cut-up olives and oregano, mix, blend, and cook for about 2 minutes. Remove garlic. Serve hot. *Serves 4.*

VEAL IN TUNA SAUCE

5 lbs. rolled boneless veal
(rump, leg or shoulder
of veal)
¼ cup olive oil
2 medium onions,
chopped
1 7½-oz. can tuna fish
1 can anchovy fillets,
minced
2 cloves garlic
2 bay leaves
½ teaspoon thyme
2 cups sauterne
rind of 1 orange
rind of 1 lemon
½ teaspoon freshly
ground black pepper
1 teaspoon salt
chicken broth
½ cup mayonnaise
capers

"Vitello Tonnato" is another delicacy from the Northern regions of Italy. It can be served as an entrée, but its succulence can best be appreciated when both meat and sauce are thoroughly chilled and served as a first course or appetizer. It keeps well for several days in the refrigerator.

Brown the veal in the olive oil. Add the onions, undrained flaked tuna fish, minced anchovies, garlic, bay leaves, thyme, wine, orange rind, lemon rind, pepper and salt. Cover and cook over low heat until veal is tender (about 25 min. per lb.); let cool in sauce. Remove the veal; discard the bay leaves, orange and lemon rind. Purée the sauce in blender. Add enough chicken broth to make 3 cups, then mix with the mayonnaise. Slice the cooled veal very thin and pour sauce over it. Garnish with capers. *Serves 6 to 8.*

STUFFED VEAL ROLLS AL MARSALA

12 small slices veal cutlet
(Italian style), cut
very thin in 4"
squares
12 small slices prosciutto
or ham, thinly sliced
12 very thin slices
mozzarella, gruyere
or Swiss cheese

2 tablespoons butter
2 tablespoons olive oil
⅓ cup Marsala or sherry
1 teaspoon butter
salt and pepper to taste

Place slice of prosciutto and a thin slice of mozzarella cheese on each slice of meat. Roll, using toothpicks to hold together. Brown rolls well on all sides in hot butter and olive oil, turning each gently, and cook until tender. Remove rolls from pan, pour in wine, and scraping bottom and sides of pan, bring to a boil. Add 1 teaspoon butter, salt and pepper, and simmer for a minute or two. Pour sauce over rolls and serve. *Serves 4.*

SALTIMBOCCA ALLA ROMANA

12 very thin slices of veal
cutlet (Italian style),
cut into 3" squares
12 thin 3" square pieces
of prosciutto or ham

sage
2 tablespoons butter
2 tablespoons olive oil
salt and pepper
¼ cup dry white wine

Literally translated, "Saltimbocca" means "jump in the mouth" —a Roman delicacy. When Queen Elizabeth visited Rome several years back she requested these famous veal tidbits and another Roman favorite "Carciofi alla Giudia"—artichokes, Jewish Style (see index).

Pound each square of veal; place one or two fresh sage leaves, or pinch of dry sage leaves, or sprinkle a little powdered sage

106

on each slice of veal and top with a piece of prosciutto. Pin prosciutto and meat together with a toothpick as you would two pieces of cloth. Brown and cook in hot butter and olive oil, first on one side with prosciutto side up, then on the other side. Sprinkle with salt and pepper to taste. Lift from pan and arrange on warm serving dish with prosciutto side up. Stir wine into drippings of pan and, scraping bottom and sides of pan, simmer for about 1 minute, then pour over "saltimbocca." *Serves 4.*

FANCY VEAL SCALOPPINE

2 cups mashed potatoes
1 egg yolk
1 tablespoon melted
　butter
pinch of nutmeg
1 egg, slightly beaten
3 tomatoes, cut in halves
4 tablespoons bread
　crumbs
1 tablespoon chopped
　parsley
1 tablespoon grated
　Parmesan cheese

olive oil
1 lb. fresh mushrooms,
　cleaned and sliced
2 tablespoons butter
3 anchovy fillets, cut up
1 to 1½ lbs. veal
　scaloppine
flour
salt and pepper
1 tablespoon butter
1 tablespoon olive oil
½ cup sherry

These scaloppine and their trimmings make a wonderful combination dish. Serve with a tossed salad for a delightfully complete meal.

Combine mashed potatoes, egg yolk, melted butter, nutmeg, salt and pepper to taste, and blend thoroughly. Shape into smooth balls and flatten out about ½" thick. Dip in flour, then in slightly beaten egg and arrange in one layer on a large greased baking pan. Remove seeds from tomato halves; mix bread crumbs, parsley and grated cheese together with a little salt and pepper to taste; sprinkle mixture over tomato halves and top with a few drops of olive oil. Place on the baking pan along with the potato cakes. Bake in a preheated 375° F. oven for about 20 to 25 minutes until tomatoes are cooked and potato cakes are golden brown, turning cakes over to brown on both sides. Meanwhile sauté mushrooms in 2 tablespoons butter for 5 to 8 minutes, then add anchovies, mix and continue cooking for another minute or two. Set aside. Dredge veal slices with flour seasoned with salt and pepper. Melt and heat 1 tablespoon butter with 1 tablespoon olive oil in a skillet and, when hot, brown veal slices on both sides over high heat, and cook until tender, about 10 minutes. Lift meat from pan and keep warm. Add sherry to pan drippings and, scraping bottom and sides of pan, cook for a minute or two. To serve: arrange slices of meat and potato cakes alternately to form a ring on a large round serving plate, each slightly overlapping the other. Fill center with the mushrooms and arrange the tomato halves around the outside of the ring. Pour the wine sauce over meat and potato cake ring. *Serves 4 to 6.*

SCALOPPINE AL MARSALA

1½ lbs. veal scaloppine	1 tablespoon olive oil
salt and pepper	1 clove garlic, crushed
2 tablespoons flour	½ cup Marsala or sherry
2 tablespoons butter	

A simple and celebrated dish with many variations. A rich sherry should be used if Marsala is not available. However, a good sauterne can be substituted. A few mushrooms, sliced and sautéed in a little butter, can be added to the pan drippings in the last step, along with the wine.

Sprinkle each piece of meat with salt and pepper, and dust with flour lightly. Melt butter and oil in large frying pan and, when hot, add clove of garlic (crushed) and veal; brown veal thoroughly on both sides over high heat, working garlic around meat (if garlic starts to burn, remove quickly). When meat is well browned, add the wine, all but 2 tablespoons, and keeping the flame high, let meat cook 1 minute longer. Arrange meat in warm serving dish. Add the remaining wine to pan, scraping bottom and sides, simmer a bit and pour over meat. *Serves 4.*

VEAL SCALOPPINE WITH PROSCIUTTO AND WINE

1 lb. veal scaloppine
2 tablespoons olive oil
2 tablespoons butter
2 tablespoons flour
¼ teaspoon pepper
½ teaspoon salt
⅛ lb. prosciutto, diced or slivered

¼ cup dry white wine
1 teaspoon butter
1 teaspoon chopped parsley
2 teaspoons lemon juice

Heat olive oil and butter in frying pan. Mix salt and pepper in flour and dredge slices of meat in flour. Sauté meat in hot butter and olive oil and cook well on each side. When meat is thoroughly cooked, remove and place on warm serving plate, and keep warm. Add prosciutto to drippings in pan, cook for about 2 minutes. Add wine, butter and parsley. Cook for about 1 minute, scraping the bottom and sides of the pan, then add lemon juice. Pour sauce over meat and serve immediately. *Serves 4.*

VEAL SHANKS ALLA MILANESE

4 veal shank bones with meat, cut 3" long (with marrow)
flour
2 tablespoons butter
2 tablespoons olive oil
salt and pepper
1 small onion, minced
1 small carrot, minced
1 small stalk celery, minced

½ cup red or white dry wine
2 tablespoons tomato paste, dissolved in ½ cup chicken broth or bouillon
3 cloves
1 small twist lemon peel
1 teaspoon butter
1 teaspoon chopped parsley

These are the celebrated "Ossobuco or Ossibuchi alla Milanese"—bearing out the fact that the meat closest to the bone is the sweetest.

Roll shanks in flour and brown evenly on all sides in hot butter and olive oil. Add onion, carrot and celery and brown well together with shanks. Moisten shanks with wine, a little at a time, and allow to evaporate somewhat. Season with salt and pepper to taste. Add dissolved tomato paste, cloves and lemon peel. Cover and simmer slowly for about 1 hour or until meat is tender. If necessary, add a little chicken broth or bouillon. When done, gently lift shanks from pan onto warm serving dish. Add the teaspoon of butter to pan sauce, stir and blend. Strain sauce over shanks and sprinkle with chopped parsley. This is served, traditionally, with Risotto alla Milanese (see page 147). *Serves 4.*

VEAL STEW WITH MARJORAM AND TOMATOES

1½ lbs. boned shoulder
   of veal, cut into large
   cubes
½ cup olive oil
2 cloves garlic
1 tablespoon chopped
   parsley

1 bay leaf
½ teaspoon marjoram
1 teaspoon salt
½ teaspoon pepper
1 cup dry white wine
1 16-oz. can tomatoes

A delicious stew which can be served over egg noodles or polenta.

Place oil in large stew-pan, add garlic and brown lightly. Remove garlic, add meat and brown thoroughly on all sides. Add parsley, bay leaf, marjoram, salt and pepper. When meat is well browned, add wine and cook slowly until it evaporates. Add tomatoes and, if necessary, enough warm water to cover meat. Cover pan, lower flame and cook slowly until meat is well done, about 30 to 45 minutes. More water may be added during cooking if necessary. *Serves 4.*

7
VEGETABLES

ARTICHOKES, JEWISH STYLE
(A ROMAN DELICACY)

"Carciofi alla Guida"—an artistic culinary creation. Figure on one or two artichokes per serving, depending on their size. size.

Choose very fresh and very green artichokes. They must be cut in a special manner: pull off just the first bottom row of tough leaves and cut off enough of the top to leave at least three inches of artichokes; with a small, very sharp knife, working from the bottom toward the top, turning artichoke slowly, taper it. In this way the thorns and the tops of tough outer leaves are tapered off, leaving all the edible parts. The artichokes should now resemble a flower. Cut off stems. Rinse artichokes in cold water to which has been added lemon juice to avoid discoloration. Drain well and dry. Holding artichoke at the bottom, tap head down on table to spread the leaves a little, then sprinkle salt and pepper inside. Place artichokes in a deep saucepan, heads down and not too close together. Cover artichokes with olive oil and let them fry slowly for several minutes over a steady medium heat. Then turn them on their sides, turning often to fry and brown evenly, especially if the olive oil does not completely cover them. When artichokes are soft to the gentle pressure of a spoon, arrange them in their former position . . . heads down.

Gently and slowly press bottoms firmly towards the bottom of the pan, raising the heat a little so that the leaves will acquire a dark golden color and become crisp. When done "il Carciofo alla Giudia" should resemble a chrysanthemum . . . rather flat with widely spread leaves. Here is a little known secret in the finishing touches of these artichokes: to give them the fried crispness (croccante) traditional to this dish, wet the hand with cold water and shake lightly over the boiling oil, spraying it; leave artichokes in the pan for another minute or two, then drain and serve hot.

ARTICHOKES ALLA ROMANA

4 artichokes, medium
    size
⅓ cup olive oil
¼ cup water
4 cloves garlic, whole
    and crushed

salt and pepper
1 teaspoon mint flakes
    (or sprig of mint
    leaves)

Cut off stems and points of the artichokes, removing tough outer leaves. Cut into quarters, removing white fuzzy fiber, or choke. Soak artichokes for a few minutes in water containing lemon juice; wash, and drain well. Place them in saucepan with oil, water, mint and garlic. Sprinkle with salt and pepper, cover and let steam slowly until tender. Serve on side dish, pouring over them some of the oil in which they have been cooked. *Serves 4.*

SAUSAGE STUFFED ARTICHOKES

4 globe artichokes
1 lb. sweet Italian
    sausages, casings
    removed
½ cup dried mushrooms
1 egg
2 tablespoons grated
    Parmesan cheese

1 tablespoon chopped
    parsley
salt and pepper
bread crumbs
butter
1 tablespoon tomato
    paste, dissolved in 1
    cup water

Soak mushrooms in a little warm water until softened; drain and chop. Cut off stems and thorny tips of artichokes. Pull off the tough bottom row of leaves and cut off one-quarter of the tops. Wash and drain. Place artichokes upright in boiling water to which a little vinegar or lemon juice has been added, and cook covered for about 20 minutes (do not overcook). Drain upside down and cool. When cooled, spread leaves apart gently, pull out the tight conical center and scrape out the choke. Prepare dressing: crumble sausage meat and sauté in a little butter until almost done; remove from heat. Add chopped mushrooms, the whole egg, grated cheese, parsley; mix and blend well, seasoning with salt and pepper to taste. Stuff artichoke centers with this dressing and push some down between the leaves. Sprinkle tops with bread crumbs, dot with butter and arrange them upright in a baking dish. Pour the dissolved tomato paste in the bottom of baking dish and bake in a preheated 375° F. oven for about 30 to 45 minutes, basting occasionally. Serve hot. *Serves 4.*

STUFFED ARTICHOKES, SICILIAN STYLE

4 large artichokes	2 tablespoons olive oil
½ cup olive oil	1 cup bread crumbs
½ medium onion, minced	2 tablespoons butter
1 clove garlic, whole and crushed	4 or 5 anchovy fillets
	¼ teaspoon pepper
1 tablespoon chopped parsley	1 cup water
	olive oil

Cut off stems (save) and tips of artichokes. Remove some of the tough outer leaves. Spread open centers and leaves of artichokes. With a small, sharp knife dig into center to remove as much as possible of the white, fuzzy fiber or choke. Wash in cold water to which has been added a little lemon juice. Drain artichokes by placing them head down. Wash and scrape stems and chop fine. Combine butter and anchovies and with a fork or blade of knife make a smooth paste. Place in a saucepan ½ cup olive oil, onion, garlic and parsley. Brown slowly until onion has acquired a dark golden color. At the same time, brown the bread crumbs in a small frying pan with 2 tablespoons olive oil. When onion has acquired a dark golden color, add toasted bread crumbs, chopped stems, anchovy paste, pepper and mix and blend ingredients well. Stuff centers and between leaves of artichokes. Arrange artichokes standing up in a baking pan. Pour 1 cup of water into the bottom of pan and pour olive oil generously over artichokes. Cover and bake in slow oven (325° F.) or on top of stove, until bottoms of artichokes are soft to the fork. Serve hot or cold on individual plates. *Serves 4.*

ASPARAGUS WITH PROSCIUTTO AU GRATIN

Figure on 5 or 6 asparagus per serving.

Wash green asparagus; cut off lower tough ends of stalks. Tie in small bunches and cook 15 minutes in large amount of rapidly boiling salted water. Lift out of water and drain thoroughly. Untie and wrap a thin slice of prosciutto or ham around 5 or 6 spears and fasten with a toothpick. Place these little bundles in a well-buttered baking pan or ovenproof dish, brush each generously with melted butter, sprinkle with grated Parmesan cheese and bake in hot 400° F. oven for 5 to 10 minutes. Remove from oven, pour more melted butter over them and serve hot.

BROCCOLI, SICILIAN STYLE

1 bunch broccoli	8 anchovy fillets, cut up
⅓ cup olive oil	½ cup grated Parmesan
1 large onion, sliced in	cheese
thin rings	salt and pepper
½ cup black sliced olives	1 cup dry red wine

Clean and wash broccoli and cut into small stalks. Grease bottom of a baking pan with a little olive oil. Arrange onions, olives, anchovies and broccoli in alternate layers in order named. Sprinkle with grated cheese, salt, pepper, and a little olive oil. Repeat procedure until ingredients are all used. Pour wine over all. Cover and place in preheated 375° F. oven for 30 to 45 minutes until broccoli is tender. *Serves 4 to 6.*

EGGPLANT WITH OLIVES IN TOMATO SAUCE

1 medium-sized eggplant
¼ cup olive oil
2 tablespoons tomato
   paste, dissolved in
   ½ cup warm water

12 black or green olives,
   pitted and cut up
1 tablespoon capers
salt and pepper

Wash and cut ends off eggplant, and without peeling, dice. Sauté in olive oil for 10 or 15 minutes until soft and tender. Add dissolved tomato paste, olives, and capers and season with salt and pepper. Mix and blend everything gently together and continue cooking for another 10 minutes until sauce thickens. Serve hot. *Serves 4.*

BAKED EGGPLANT PARMESAN

2 medium-sized
   eggplants
flour
1 or 2 eggs, slightly
   beaten
½ teaspoon salt
¼ teaspoon pepper
1 cup olive oil

¼ cup grated Parmesan
   cheese
½ to 1 lb. mozzarella
   cheese, sliced thin
tomato sauce (see page
   188) or "Quick Sauce"
   (see page 189)

Peel eggplant, cut into ¼ inch slices. Sprinkle each slice with salt; pile slices between two plates, topped with a weight to draw out juices; let stand 1 hour. Pat slices dry, dredge in flour and dip in egg. Fry in hot olive oil until slices are golden brown on both sides. Drain on paper. Spread a thin layer of sauce in the bottom of a casserole, top with a layer of eggplant slices, cover with a layer of sauce, sprinkle with grated cheese and top with a layer of mozzarella slices. Repeat this procedure until all eggplant is used, ending with mozzarella. Bake in a preheated 400° F. oven for 15 to 20 minutes, or until cheese is melted, and serve. *Serves 4 to 6.*

EGGPLANT SANDWICHES

2 medium-sized
    eggplants
1 cup flour
1½ cups olive oil
3 egg yolks
¼ lb. mozzarella cheese,
    diced fine or grated

2 tablespoons grated
    Parmesan cheese
pinch of salt
2 eggs, lightly beaten
1 cup bread crumbs

Cut off ends, peel eggplant and slice in ½-inch rounds. Dust in flour and fry slightly in hot olive oil. Set aside, draining on paper. Save the oil. In a bowl mix together well the egg yolks, mozzarella, grated cheese and salt, to obtain a thick paste-like mixture. Form "sandwiches" by joining two slices of eggplant, placing a tablespoon of the cheese mixture between each pair. Dip each sandwich into beaten eggs, then in bread crumbs and fry in hot olive oil until golden brown on both sides. Serve hot. *Serves 4 to 6.*

STUFFED EGGPLANT TIMBALE

3 or 4 medium-sized
    eggplants
½ cup olive oil or fat
2 cups leftover cooked
    beef, veal or chicken,
    or a mixture of all
1 lb. sweet Italian
    sausages
3 tablespoons butter

2 small onions, minced
1 clove garlic, minced
2 small tomatoes, peeled
    and chopped
2 tablespoons chopped
    parsley
salt and pepper
2 eggs, slightly beaten

This succulent entrée of Greek origin is well worth the effort.

Wash and dry eggplants and remove stems. Cut in two lengthwise and sauté in olive oil, pulp side down, until softened, about 10 minutes. Lift from pan, scoop out pulp, leaving skins intact; carefully flatten skins. Chop pulp and set aside. Meanwhile remove casings from sausages, crumble meat and sauté in 1 tablespoon butter until tender. Blend in leftover meat and remove from heat. Add 2 tablespoons butter to drippings in pan where eggplants were cooked and brown onion and garlic lightly. Add eggplant pulp and tomatoes and cook until eggplant is tender, stirring often. Add parsley, salt and pepper to taste. Blend in sausage mixture. Remove from heat, add eggs to bind mixture, blending well. Butter or oil a timbale mold and line it with the eggplant skins (cut side up), each slightly overlapping the other lengthwise, meeting at the center of pan and letting ends hang about 2 or 3 inches over sides of pan. Fill lined mold with mixture and fold skins over it so they will meet in the center over top. Place timbale in a pan of hot water and bake in moderate 375° F. oven for 45 to 60 minutes or until firm. Unmold on warm serving platter and pour a thick tomato sauce over it and serve immediately. *Serves 4 to 6.*

GREEN BEANS IN TOMATO SAUCE

1 lb. fresh green beans	1 16-oz. can tomatoes
6 tablespoons olive oil	1 teaspoon salt
1 clove garlic, sliced	¼ teaspoon pepper

Cut off both ends of beans, wash and drain, and French, or cut on the slant. Heat olive oil in saucepan and brown garlic very slightly, a light golden color; add tomatoes, salt and pepper, and crush tomatoes with wooden fork. Cook for 5 minutes, then add string beans, mix thoroughly with tomatoes, cover and let simmer slowly until beans are tender and sauce has thickened. *Serves 4.*

LENTILS, HOME STYLE

3 cups lentils
¼ onion, chopped
2 or 3 slices prosciutto,
    ham or bacon
1 teaspoon butter

2 tablespoons olive oil
½ 16-oz. can tomatoes,
    drained
salt and pepper to taste
1 cup chicken broth

Cook lentils in salted water until tender but firm about 10 to 15 minutes. (Do not overcook.) Drain well. Brown onion and prosciutto in butter and olive oil in deep saucepan, large enough to hold lentils. When onion has acquired a slightly golden color, add tomatoes, crush with fork, add salt and pepper to taste. Mix ingredients well together and add broth. Let simmer for a minute or two, then add lentils and cook gently, mixing lightly, until lentils have absorbed the broth. Serve as a side dish for meat, ham or sausage. *Serves 4 to 6.*

STUFFED LETTUCE LEAVES

1 or 2 sweet Italian
    sausages
½ clove garlic, minced
2 tablespoons chopped
    parsley
1 tablespoon butter
1 tablespoon olive oil
2 cups chopped leftover
    cooked meat, chicken
    or turkey
1 cup chopped lettuce
½ cup broth or bouillon

2 tablespoons bread
    crumbs
2 tablespoons grated
    Parmesan cheese
1 egg, slightly beaten
12 large lettuce leaves
1 small onion, chopped
2 tablespoons butter
2 tablespoons tomato
    paste, dissolved in 1
    cup warm broth

Remove casings from sausages and crumble meat. In a frying pan brown the garlic and parsley very lightly in 1 tablespoon butter and 1 tablespoon olive oil. When garlic has just started to color, add chopped meat, sausage and chopped lettuce and brown for a few minutes, mixing and blending. Add ½ cup warm broth and bring to a boil. Then add bread crumbs, remove from fire, mix and blend everything well together and let cool. Add cheese and egg and mix well. Dip and scald lettuce leaves in boiling salted water, removing quickly and spreading each one separately on work board. On each lettuce leaf place a little mound of meat mixture, roll leaf over filling, turning ends under so as to secure each roll into a little bundle and fasten if necessary with a toothpick; set aside. Brown onion in 2 tablespoons butter, add the lettuce bundles and gently brown each one on all sides. Then add the dissolved tomato paste, bring to a boil and let simmer for about 20 minutes. Serve hot. *Serves 4.*

STUFFED MUSHROOMS WITH RICOTTA

12 large fresh mushrooms	salt and pepper
1 slice white bread,	2 eggs
broken in small pieces	½ to 1 cup ricotta cheese
2 cloves garlic, minced	grated Parmesan cheese
½ tablespoon chopped	olive oil
parsley	

Remove stems from mushrooms. Wash mushrooms and dry. Clean stems and chop fine. Combine chopped stems, bread, garlic, parsley, eggs, ricotta, salt and pepper, and mix together well. Fill each mushroom cap with stuffing, heaping stuffing on top. Sprinkle with grated cheese. Arrange mushrooms in a greased baking pan (use olive oil) and bake in preheated 350° F. oven for about 30 minutes. *Serves 4 to 6.*

MUSHROOMS IN TOMATO SAUCE

1 lb. large mushrooms
3 tablespoons olive oil
4 anchovy fillets, cut up
2 cloves garlic (whole)
2 fresh ripe tomatoes

pinch of dry mint leaves
salt and pepper
bread triangles, fried in
    olive oil or toasted

Plunge tomatoes in boiling water for a few minutes until skin peels easily. Peel and cut into small pieces. Heat olive oil in a skillet, add mushrooms, well cleaned and cut into large slices, anchovies, garlic, tomatoes and mint. Season with salt and pepper to taste. Cover and let cook briskly over high heat, stirring occasionally, for 15 to 20 minutes. Serve garnished with fried bread. *Serves 4 to 6.*

ARTICHOKE AND SHRIMP STUFFED ONIONS

4 large onions
4 artichoke hearts
    (canned or frozen),
    chopped
8 fresh shrimp, shelled,
    deveined and cut up
6 anchovy fillets, cut up
4 tablespoons butter

2 tablespoons flour
¾ cup milk
2 egg yolks
salt and pepper to taste
dash of cayenne
bread crumbs
dots of butter

Remove skins from onions and parboil in salted water, uncovered, for about 8 minutes. Drain and turn upside down to cool. Remove centers of onions, leaving a shell sufficiently thick to retain its shape. Chop a third of the onion centers and sauté in 2 tablespoons butter, adding artichoke hearts, shrimp and anchovies. Season with salt and pepper. Meanwhile prepare cream sauce: melt 2 tablespoons butter, stir in flour, add milk gradually and let thicken, stirring constantly. Remove from heat and stir in egg yolks, one at a time, mixing and blending well after each addition. Season with salt and pepper and a dash of cayenne. Add shrimp and artichoke mixture to cream sauce; blend well. Stuff onion shells; sprinkle with bread crumbs and place a dot of butter on each. Bake in a well-greased baking pan in a preheated 350° F. oven for about 30 minutes. Perfect as a hot appetizer or served with meat, fish or fowl. *Serves 4.*

PEAS, ROMAN STYLE

1 can peas, drained	stock or chicken broth or
2 tablespoons butter	bouillon
½ onion, sliced	salt and pepper
2 or 3 slices prosciutto, cut in slivers	

Melt butter in saucepan, sauté onion and prosciutto, add peas, a small amount of stock or chicken broth (or water), salt and pepper; let simmer until peas are thoroughly heated. (If fresh peas are used, cover with enough stock or broth, simmer until tender and stock or broth is absorbed.) *Serves 2 to 4.*

PEPPERS IN PIQUANT SAUCE

6 large sweet green peppers	1 teaspoon oregano
3 tablespoons olive oil	2 tablespoons capers
4 whole peeled canned tomatoes	

Cut peppers in halves, remove veins and seeds and cut into quarters or eighths. Place in deep frying pan or shallow saucepan with olive oil and sauté until softened. Add the tomatoes, cut up or crushed, the capers and mix. Sprinkle with oregano and let cook gently for another 15 or 20 minutes until tender and serve. *Serves 4.*

STUFFED PEPPERS, NEAPOLITAN STYLE

4 sweet peppers, medium size
½ cup olive oil
2 cups bread crumbs
2 tablespoons raisins, soaked in warm water
6 anchovy fillets, cut up
20 ripe olives, pitted and chopped
1 tablespoon chopped parsley

1 tablespoon chopped fresh basil (or 1 teaspoon dried basil)
2 tablespoons capers
¼ teaspoon pepper
salt to taste
4 teaspoons olive oil
½ cup "Quick" tomato sauce (see page 189)

Cut off tops of peppers, remove seeds and veins, and wash. Heat olive oil in frying pan, add bread crumbs and, mixing gently with wooden spoon, brown lightly. Remove from heat, add raisins, anchovies, olives, parsley, basil, capers and pepper. Salt to taste if necessary. Mix thoroughly and, if mixture seems too dry, add more oil. Fill peppers with mixture. Select a baking dish or casserole just large enough to hold peppers standing up close together, and cover bottom with olive oil. Arrange peppers in pan; pour a teaspoon of olive oil over each pepper and top each with 1 tablespoon "Quick" tomato sauce. Bake in preheated 375° F. oven for about 45 minutes or until peppers are done. Can be served hot or cold. *Serves 4.*

UPSIDE DOWN STUFFED BAKED PEPPERS

5 sweet green peppers, medium size	2 tablespoons chopped parsley
½ cup olive oil	1 teaspoon chopped basil
1 clove garlic, whole and crushed	8 ripe olives, pitted and sliced
1 fresh tomato, peeled and cut up	4 anchovy fillets, cut up
1 cup bread crumbs	4 slices toast

Roast 1 pepper in a hot 450° F. oven or under a broiler for about 10 minutes or until skin is easily removed. Peel, remove seeds and cut into slivers. Cover tomato with boiling water for a few minutes until skin is easily removed. Peel and cut up in small pieces, crushing a bit. Place garlic, olive oil, tomato and slivered pepper in saucepan or skillet and sauté for a few minutes until garlic begins to color. Remove garlic. Add bread crumbs, mix and blend well for a minute or two. Remove pan from stove, add parsley, basil, olives and anchovies; mix and blend all ingredients well. If too dry, add a little olive oil. Prepare peppers for stuffing by cutting all around stem with a sharp knife and removing it, remove seeds, leaving pepper intact. Stuff peppers with mixture. Place a slice of toast on top of each pepper and arrange peppers upside down (open side down on toast) in a baking dish. Pour a little olive oil over each and bake in preheated 350° F. oven for about 45 minutes. Baste 2 or 3 times with juices in pan. *Serves 4.*

SPINACH TOSSED IN OLIVE OIL AND GARLIC

2 lbs. spinach	salt
¼ cup olive oil	pinch red pepper seeds (optional)
1 clove garlic, whole and crushed	

"Spinaci Saltati"—a quick and delicious hot dressing for spinach.

Cook spinach until tender (don't overcook). Drain thoroughly until dry. In a frying pan brown garlic in olive oil. When it begins to color (don't burn), add spinach, tossing gently, adding salt and pepper seeds. Sauté for a few minutes and serve hot. *Serves 4.*

SPINACH IN TOMATO SAUCE

¼ cup dried mushrooms
2 tablespoons chopped
onion
2 tablespoons butter
¼ clove garlic
1 tablespoon chopped
parsley

2 lbs. spinach, cleaned
and cut up
1 tablespoon tomato
paste, dissolved in
1½ cups warm water
salt and pepper

Soak mushrooms in 1 cup warm water for ½ hour, drain and chop. Brown onion lightly in hot butter, add garlic, parsley and mushrooms and continue browning for a few minutes longer. Add spinach and dissolved tomato paste. Season with salt and a little pepper, mix, and let simmer gently for about 15 to 20 minutes. This is a delightful dish garnished with sliced hard-cooked eggs. *Serves 4 to 6.*

EGGPLANT STUFFED TOMATOES

4 large firm tomatoes
1 medium eggplant
2 tablespoons chopped
parsley
2 cloves garlic, chopped
fine

mozzarella cheese, cut in
very thin slices
olive oil
salt and pepper

129

Wash eggplant; cut ends off; do not peel. Cut 4 very thin lengthwise slices from eggplant. (Rest of eggplant may be put to some other use.) Sprinkle each slice with salt and set aside to drain for about 30 minutes. Cut a slice from the top of each tomato and scoop out pulp. Season inside of tomato cases with salt and pepper. Mix parsley and garlic together. Pat dry eggplant slices; flatten them out. Sprinkle each slice with parsley and garlic mixture, top with thin slices of mozzarella and roll tightly, fastening with a toothpick if necessary. Place each roll inside a tomato case, standing up. Arrange stuffed tomatoes in an oiled baking pan, drizzle each generously with olive oil and bake in a preheated 350° F. oven for 40 to 60 minutes, or until both vegetables are cooked. Serve hot. *Serves 4.*

MIXED VEGETABLE FRY

BATTER

2 eggs
⅔ cup milk
1 tablespoon olive oil
1 tablespoon grated
    Parmesan cheese
1 cup sifted flour
½ teaspoon salt

fat or olive oil for deep
    frying

cauliflower flowerlets
celery stalks, cut into 2"
    or 3" pieces

asparagus spears
artichokes, cleaned and
    cut into thin slices
green beans
broccoli, cut into small
    stalks
green peppers, quartered
zucchini, cut ¼" thick in
    lengthwise slices, then
    into 2" or 3" pieces
eggplant, cut same as
    zucchini
spinach sprigs

A mixed vegetable fry is a combination of different vegetables dipped in batter and fried in hot fat. Vegetables should be lightly parboiled first (not overcooked), with the exception of

*zucchini, eggplant and spinach. Canned or frozen vegetables
may be used; in that case, there is no need to parboil.*

Prepare Batter: Beat eggs until thick and lemon colored; add
milk, olive oil; blend well. Stir in cheese, flour and salt and
mix until well blended. Batter should be just thick enough to
coat vegetables well. Dip vegetables in batter and fry in deep
hot fat until golden. Serve hot with lemon wedges. Vegetables
may also be sprinkled with a little lemon juice before dipping
in batter. A combination of any of the above vegetables or
one type of vegetable, prepared as above, makes a delicious
accompaniment to meat, fish or fowl.

FRIED ZUCCHINI, JULIENNE

Select firm medium-sized zucchini (Italian squash). Wash and
cut ends off. Cut ¼ inch thick in lengthwise slices, then into
matchlike strips. Sprinkle with salt, place in colander or large
strainer to enable liquid from zucchini to drain; let stand for
one hour. When ready to fry take a few at a time, squeeze
lightly, dredge in flour and shake in a strainer to remove ex-
cess flour. Fry a few at a time in deep hot olive oil or fat until
crisp and a very light golden brown. Serve piled high on warm
serving dish, garnished with lemon wedges. Serve these delicious Julienne zucchini in place of French fried potatoes. (Four
or 5 medium-sized zucchini will serve 4 to 6.)

PAN-COOKED ZUCCHINI WITH CHEESE

4 medium zucchini
1 clove garlic, whole and
   crushed
3 tablespoons olive oil
1 tablespoon chopped
   parsley

salt and pepper to taste
1 tablespoon grated
   Parmesan cheese
1 cup mozzarella, or
   Swiss cheese, grated
   coarsely

Clean zucchini and slice in 1- or 1½-inch pieces, and sauté in olive oil with garlic, parsley, salt and pepper for about 10 minutes. Sprinkle with grated Parmesan cheese and add the mozzarella cheese, cover and cook slowly for another 5 or 10 minutes or until tender and cheese has melted. Serve hot. *Serves 4.*

ZUCCHINI IN TOMATO SAUCE

4 to 6 small zucchini
1 teaspoon butter
1 tablespoon olive oil
2 slices lean bacon, cut
   up

¼ small onion, chopped
½ 16-oz. can tomatoes

Lightly scrape zucchini, wash and cut into cubes. Sprinkle cubes with salt and let stand for about an hour. Then brown bacon and onion in hot butter and olive oil and when lightly colored add zucchini; sauté for a few minutes, then add tomatoes, mix and let simmer gently until zucchini are tender, and sauce thickened. *Serves 4.*

TUNA STUFFED ZUCCHINI

6 small zucchini
1 tablespoon olive oil
1 tablespoon butter
2 tablespoons chopped
    parsley
½ clove garlic, minced
2 peeled canned
    tomatoes, cut up
½ cup tuna fish, chopped

2 tablespoons bread
    crumbs
2 tablespoons grated
    Parmesan cheese
1 or 2 eggs, slightly
    beaten
butter and olive oil
bread crumbs

Select firm zucchini. Cut off ends, scrape slightly and wash. Parboil for about 3 minutes and drain. Cut in half lengthwise. Scoop out pulp and save. Brown parsley and garlic with 1 tablespoon of olive oil and 1 tablespoon butter. When garlic is lightly browned, add zucchini pulp, tomatoes and tuna fish and let simmer for a few minutes, mixing and blending ingredients. Add bread crumbs, let thicken and remove from heat. When cooled add grated cheese and eggs and blend everything well together. Butter bottom of a baking pan and add 2 tablespoons of olive oil. Fill zucchini cases with tuna mixture and arrange side by side in pan. Sprinkle with bread crumbs and olive oil. Bake in moderate 375° F. oven for about 45 minutes. Serve hot. *Serves 6.*

8
POTATOES

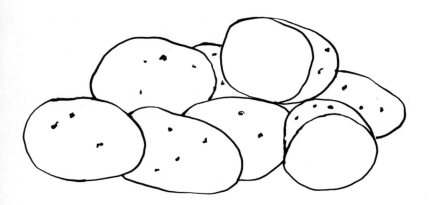

STUFFED BAKED POTATOES

4 medium-sized raw potatoes	1 teaspoon capers
2 tablespoons olive oil	3 anchovy fillets, cut up
½ onion, minced	Pinch of pepper
4 or 5 canned tomatoes, drained	1 cup diced mozzarella or Swiss cheese
½ teaspoon chopped basil	olive oil
½ teaspoon chopped parsley	

A novel way of stuffing potatoes—attractive and delicious.

Select potatoes that are well-rounded and of even size. Peel and then cut a thin slice off one end in order to make each potato stand up. Cut a ¼-inch slice off the top end of each potato and save. Scoop out insides carefully with an apple corer. Place oil and onion in small frying pan and brown lightly, add tomatoes and cook over high heat for a few minutes, being careful not to crush tomatoes too much. Remove pan from fire, add basil, parsley, capers, anchovies, pepper and mozzarella. Mix gently. Stuff the potato cases with this mixture. Pour oil from pan over stuffing into each potato. Cover each potato with its top slice and seal the tops to the potatoes with a paste made by combining 1½ teaspoons flour with a little egg white. Place potatoes standing up in baking dish or pan, pour olive oil over them and bake in preheated 375° F. oven for 45 minutes. Do not open oven too often during baking process because air will crack potatoes. Serve hot! *Serves 4.*

POTATO CROQUETTES

3 cups mashed cooked
    potatoes
2 tablespoons grated
    cheese
1 tablespoon chopped
    parsley

1 egg
flour
1 or 2 eggs, beaten lightly
bread crumbs
1 cup olive oil

Mix mashed potatoes with a little butter, milk, salt and pepper. Add grated cheese, parsley and egg to mashed potatoes, mixing and blending thoroughly; chill. Shape into croquettes the size of small eggs. Dip in flour, then in egg, and roll in bread crumbs. Fry in hot olive oil until brown on all sides. Serve hot. *Serves 4.*

POTATO BRIOCHES

1 lb. potatoes
2 tablespoons butter
salt and pepper to taste
pinch of nutmeg
1 egg yolk
mozzarella, Swiss or Ched-
    dar cheese, cut into 1″
    cubes

1 egg, beaten lightly
2 tablespoons fine bread
    crumbs

Peel potatoes, slice and boil in water 15 minutes, or until tender. Drain, mash or put through ricer, add butter, salt, pepper and nutmeg and mix well. Add egg yolk, mix and blend. Grease about 6 or 8 muffin tins or small molds. Fill three-quarters full with the potato mixture, press one cube mozzarella cheese into center of each. Brush top with egg, sprinkle with bread crumbs and bake in hot oven (about 400° F.) approximately 25 minutes. Unmold immediately and serve.

POTATO PIZZA

1 lb. potatoes
1 cup flour
½ teaspoon salt
olive oil
3 or 4 peeled canned toma-
    toes, drained and cut
    in slivers

½ lb. mozzarella, diced
2 tablespoons grated
    Parmesan cheese
pinch of pepper
1 tablespoon oregano

Boil potatoes in their jackets, until tender. Peel and mash, gradually adding the flour and salt, blending ingredients well together. Grease a 10-inch pie dish or pizza pan with olive oil and spread potato mixture on bottom about ½ or 1 inch thick. Arrange diced mozzarella evenly over top, sprinkle with grated cheese, pepper and oregano. Top with slivers of tomato and sprinkle a little olive oil over all. Bake in preheated hot 400° F. oven for about 30 minutes or until cheese has melted and is slightly browned and the pie lightly crisp. *Serves 4.*

STUFFED POTATO TIMBALE, GOURMET

2 to 2½ lbs. potatoes
2 tablespoons grated
    Parmesan cheese
1 tablespoon butter
2 eggs
pinch of nutmeg
salt and pepper
½ lb. leftover cooked
    meat, chicken or
    turkey
¼ lb. mozzarella cheese,
    or fontina

⅛ lb. Swiss cheese
⅛ lb. prosciutto or ham
1 16-oz. can whole peeled
    tomatoes
1 tablespoon olive oil
1 teaspoon butter
½ onion, chopped
1 teaspoon basil
salt and pepper
grated cheese
bread crumbs

139

A delicious harmony of ingredients makes this a marvelous entrée.

Boil potatoes with their jackets in salted water until tender. Peel and mash or pass through ricer. Place in a bowl, add grated cheese, eggs, and 1 tablespoon of butter, mixing and blending well; season with salt, pepper and nutmeg. Meanwhile empty can of tomatoes in a saucepan, add olive oil, 1 teaspoon butter, onion, basil, salt and pepper; bring to boil, lower heat and simmer for about 15 to 20 minutes. Then press through a sieve into a bowl and set aside. Cut leftover meat, the cheeses and the prosciutto into small, thin slices and keep separate. Generously butter a 2 quart round mold or deep baking dish and sprinkle heavily with bread crumbs so as to have a good solid lining. Carefully line bottom and sides of mold thickly with two-thirds of the potato mixture. Arrange over potato mixture, in layers, first the meat, then the Swiss cheese, half the prosciutto, then mozzarella cheese and the remaining prosciutto; spreading each layer with 2 or 3 table-spoons tomato sauce and a light sprinkling of grated cheese. Cover filling with remaining potato mixture, pressing with fingers gently all around edge and center. Sprinkle with bread crumbs and dot with butter. Bake in preheated moderate 350° F. oven for 20 or 25 minutes, remove from oven and let stand for 10 minutes, not more. Then unmold on serving plate and spread remaining tomato sauce over mold, or serve separately. *Serves 6.*

9
RICE

CHEESE STUFFED RICE BALLS

4 cups cooked rice
½ cup grated Parmesan
  cheese
3 tablespoons butter,
  melted
1 egg, well beaten

salt and pepper to taste
mozzarella cheese, cut into
  ¾" or 1" cubes
bread crumbs
olive oil for deep frying

Prepare these well ahead of time, refrigerate, then drop in hot olive oil and fry to a golden brown . . . serve immediately.

Mix rice with grated Parmesan cheese, melted butter; add egg and season. Blend and chill. Shape chilled rice into patties, in the palm of your hand, and place a cube of mozzarella in the center, then shape into balls, completely covering the cheese with the rice. Roll in bread crumbs and fry in hot olive oil until golden brown on all sides. Makes about 8 to 10 rice balls. *Serves 4 to 6.*

RICE AND MEAT CROQUETTES

3 cups cooked rice
1 tablespoon melted
  butter
2 tablespoons grated
  Parmesan cheese
½ cup chopped leftover
  cooked meat

1 egg
½ cup flour
1 or 2 eggs, slightly beaten
1 cup bread crumbs
1 cup olive oil

Combine first 5 ingredients and mix thoroughly. Shape into croquettes the size of small eggs. Dip in flour, then in egg, roll in bread crumbs and fry in deep hot olive oil until brown on all sides. Serve hot. Makes 6 to 8 croquettes. *Serves 4.*

RICE AND CAULIFLOWER

1½ cups raw rice
1 small cauliflower
juice of 1 lemon
4 tablespoons butter
1 onion, minced

1 teaspoon tomato paste
1½ quarts boiling broth
(approximately)
4 tablespoons grated
Parmesan cheese

This delicious "Risotto" is usually served as a first course but it can be served with meat, fish or fowl.

Remove leaves from cauliflower, cut off stalk and soak (head down) in cold salted water. Drain. Separate flowerettes, drop into boiling water with lemon juice and parboil for about five minutes. Drain, rinse in cold water and drain thoroughly. Brown the onion in 2 tablespoons butter until soft; add the tomato paste, dissolved in ½ cup broth. Cover and let simmer for about 10 minutes. Then stir in the rice and cauliflower and enough broth to cover. Season with salt to taste and bring to boil, cover, lower heat and simmer for 15 to 20 minutes or until rice is tender, yet firm. Rice should absorb the broth in cooking; if necessary, add more broth now and then. Stir occasionally to keep from sticking to pan. When rice is done, add the remaining 2 tablespoons butter and the grated cheese. Mix and blend well until butter is dissolved, and serve hot. *Serves 4 to 6.*

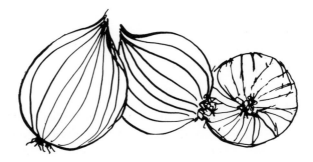

RICE WITH EGGPLANT, PARMESAN

2 medium-sized eggplants
½ cup olive oil
3 tablespoons olive oil
1 tablespoon butter
3 slices prosciutto, minced
½ small onion, chopped
1½ 6-oz. cans tomato
　　paste
salt and pepper to taste
2 cups warm water

1 lb. raw rice (2 cups)
warm broth, bouillon or
　　water
2 tablespoons butter
2 oz. grated Parmesan
　　cheese
½ lb. mozzarella cheese,
　　sliced thin
1 teaspoon chopped basil

Served with a tossed green salad, this is a complete meal.

Peel eggplant, slice in thin lengthwise pieces and fry in ½ cup olive oil until golden on both sides. As slices are done, remove, drain on paper and sprinkle with salt. In a saucepan place 3 tablespoons olive oil, 1 tablespoon butter and prosciutto. Heat. When hot, add onion and brown thoroughly. Stir in tomato paste, salt and pepper, mixing and blending well. Add 2 cups warm water and cook until sauce thickens. Remove 1 cup of sauce from pan and set aside. Clean and wash rice, add to sauce in saucepan, mixing well. Add enough warm broth, a little at a time, for rice to cook in and yet not become dry. Add broth as needed until rice is tender and has absorbed sauce. When done, add 1 tablespoon butter and 2 tablespoons of grated cheese and mix well. Place half the rice in a buttered, deep baking dish or pan, then arrange half the eggplant slices over the rice. Cover with half the mozzarella slices, spread half of the reserved tomato sauce. Sprinkle with grated cheese, chopped basil, and dot with butter here and there. Cover with the remaining rice and eggplant; top with remaining slices of the mozzarella. Spread the reserved sauce over all and sprinkle with grated cheese. Place in hot oven (about 400° F.) and bake for about 15 minutes or until mozzarella is melted. *Serves 6.*

RICE WITH FRESH TOMATO SAUCE

1½ cups raw rice
1 medium onion, chopped
2 tablespoons butter
2 tablespoons olive oil
1 lb. tomatoes, peeled and
chopped

salt and pepper
1 quart hot broth, bouillon or water, or more
as needed
grated Parmesan cheese

A delicious "Risotto" cooked in a delightfully seasoned fresh tomato broth.

Pick and wash rice, drain dry. Brown onion in butter and olive oil in deep pan. Add tomatoes, salt and pepper and cook gently until tomatoes are tender, about 15 minutes. Add broth, bring to boil and stir in rice. Cover and cook gently until rice is tender and has absorbed the liquid. Add 3 or 4 tablespoons grated cheese, mix and blend. Remove from heat and serve hot. *Serves 4 to 6.*

RICE WITH MUSHROOMS ALLA FEDORA

1½ cups raw rice
2 ounces sweet butter (¼ cup)
1 small onion, minced
½ lb. Italian sweet sausage, skinned and minced
½ cup dried mushrooms, softened in warm water, drained and minced

1 lb. fresh mushrooms
3 tablespoons butter
grated Parmesan cheese
1 quart boiling chicken broth (approximately)
salt and pepper to taste

My V.I.P. offering at a dinner party—a gastronomic treat. This is always served as a first course.

Pick over rice, put in strainer and rinse thoroughly under running cold water, rubbing between fingers until all starch has been removed; let drain and dry thoroughly. Melt ¼ cup butter in deep saucepan, add onion and brown until light golden in color; add rice and sear until light golden, stirring constantly. Add sausage and brown with rice for a minute or two. Stir in dried mushrooms, then add broth, a little at a time, stirring constantly. Add enough broth to cover rice. Add salt and pepper to taste, bring to boil, cover and cook slowly 15 to 20 minutes or until rice is tender, yet firm. Rice should absorb the broth in cooking. Do not let rice become too dry; if necessary, add more broth. Stir frequently to keep from sticking to pan. While rice is cooking, clean, wash and slice fresh mushrooms and sauté gently in 3 tablespoons butter in a frying pan, until tender. When rice is done, stir in two tablespoons grated cheese. Remove from fire, arrange on a serving platter and make a slight groove lengthwise in center, into which heap the sautéed mushrooms. Sprinkle generously with more grated cheese. Serve hot! *Serves 4.*

RISOTTO ALLA MILANESE

1½ cups rice
½ cup sweet butter (¼ lb.)
1 medium onion, minced fine
5 cups (approximately) hot chicken broth or bouillon

salt to taste
⅛ teaspoon saffron, dissolved in 2 tablespoons of broth
⅓ cup grated Parmesan cheese

The international fame of this simple rice dish attests to its gastronomical delight. For a richer bouquet try adding 2 or 3 tablespoons of dry white wine while rice is sautéing in the onion and butter.

Pick over rice, put in a fine strainer and rinse thoroughly under running cold water. Drain well and let dry. In a deep saucepan sauté onion in hot melted butter until soft and transparent (do not allow to brown); slowly stir in rice and sauté to a light golden color, stirring constantly. Stir in broth gradually. Season to taste, lower heat, cover and simmer gently for 15 to 20 minutes or until rice is tender, yet firm and has absorbed the broth. Stir often. Do not allow rice to become dry—add more broth as needed. When done, stir in dissolved saffron and blend well. Remove from heat, fold in grated cheese and serve steaming hot with more grated cheese sprinkled generously over it. For "Risotto alla Piemontese" (Piedmont) omit saffron, and top with thin slices of white truffles. *Serves 4.*

RICE WITH SHRIMP SAUCE, ADRIATIC

SAUCE	SHRIMP STOCK
1½ to 2 lbs. shrimp	shrimp shells and tails
¼ cup olive oil	2 tablespoons olive oil
1 tablespoon butter	½ onion, chopped
½ onion, minced	½ carrot, chopped
salt and pepper	½ stalk celery, chopped
½ cup Marsala or sherry	1 clove garlic (whole)
2 tablespoons tomato	¼ cup dry white wine
paste (optional)	1½ quarts hot water
1 lb. rice, about 2 cups	½ teaspoon salt
hot shrimp stock or water	
2 tablespoons butter	
grated Parmesan cheese	

From the Italian shores of the Adriatic comes this superb risotto cooked in a flavorful shrimp stock. The little effort involved is well worth the result. For full enjoyment serve it separately as a first course.

Wash shrimp. Split along back, remove shells and tails; devein. Set cleaned shrimp aside. Prepare shrimp stock: break up shells and tails into small pieces and place in saucepan with olive oil, onion, carrot, celery and garlic and brown everything well together. Add wine and let evaporate. Add water and salt, bring to boil, lower heat and simmer for 30 minutes; strain. Prepare sauce: sauté onion gently in olive oil and butter until soft, add shrimp and sauté slowly for about 5 minutes, seasoning with salt and pepper. Add Marsala and let evaporate. Add tomato paste (if desired), dissolved in a little shrimp stock, mix and continue cooking for another 2 or 3 minutes. Add rice and enough shrimp stock to cover. Bring to boil and cook over low heat until rice is tender (about 15 to 20 minutes) and has absorbed the stock. If necessary, add more stock as needed. Don't overcook rice or let it become too dry. When done, add 2 tablespoons butter and 2 tablespoons grated cheese, remove from fire, mix lightly until butter has melted and serve hot. *Serves 6.*

10
PASTA

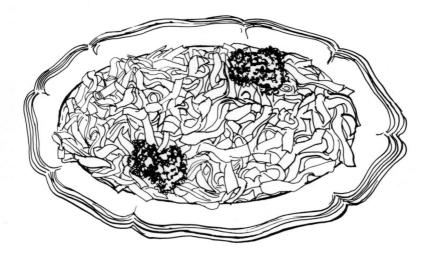

BAKED LASAGNE

tomato sauce with
chopped meat (see
recipe, page 184)

LASAGNE

1 lb. lasagne
5 quarts water
1 tablespoon salt
1 tablespoon olive oil

FILLING

1 lb. mozzarella cheese,
sliced thin
1 lb. ricotta
½ cup grated Parmesan
cheese

These famous Neapolitan "Lasagne Imbotite" can also be dressed with a plain tomato sauce, see page 188.

Bring 5 quarts of water to boil, add oil, salt and lasagne and cook from 10 to 20 minutes, or until tender, stirring frequently to prevent sticking together. Drain and rinse in cold water; drain again. Spread a thin layer of sauce in a rectangular baking pan; arrange lasagne strips in layers, side by side—3 or 4 strips to each layer. Spread each layer of lasagne with ricotta, topping with slices of mozzarella, spread with a layer of sauce and sprinkle with grated cheese. Repeat this procedure until ingredients are all used. Top last layer with sauce and grated cheese. Bake in a preheated 375° F. oven for about 30 minutes or until mozzarella is melted. This is a basic baked lasagne recipe and to embellish it any of the following or a combination of them may be added to the layers: sliced hard-cooked eggs, cooked peas, tiny meatballs or thin slices of cooked Italian sausages. *Serves 6 to 8.*

BAKED LASAGNE WITH SPINACH AND CHICKEN LIVER SAUCE

1 lb. lasagne
1 lb. cooked spinach, chopped fine
1 lb. ricotta cheese
grated Parmesan cheese

SAUCE

4 tablespoons butter
1 small onion, chopped fine
1 stalk celery, chopped fine
1 carrot, chopped fine
1 clove
¼ cup dried mushrooms

½ lb. ground lean pork or veal
½ lb. ground beef
1 teaspoon tomato paste, dissolved in 1 cup water
salt and pepper to taste
2½ cups milk
10 to 12 chicken livers, cut up
2 tablespoons butter
2 tablespoons sherry
1 tablespoon flour mixed with ¼ cup cream

Be generous with the Parmesan cheese in this famous Bolognese Lasagne dish!

Soak mushrooms in a little warm water to soften for about ½ hour; drain well and chop fine. *Prepare Sauce*: place butter, onion, celery, carrot, clove, chopped mushrooms, pork and beef in saucepan. Mixing and blending, brown ingredients together over high heat until well-colored. Stir in dissolved tomato paste, season with salt and pepper to taste. Lower heat and let simmer gently for about 1 hour, adding milk, a little at a time, during cooking process. About 15 or 20 minutes before sauce is done, sauté chicken livers in hot butter, over high heat, and add sherry; let sherry evaporate. Remove pan from heat, season livers with salt to taste and keep warm. Stir flour and cream mixture into simmering sauce and continue cooking for another ten minutes. Remove sauce from heat; blend in chicken livers. Meanwhile cook lasagne in boiling salted water until tender. Drain, rinse in cold water to prevent lasagne from sticking together and drain again. Combine ricotta and spinach, blending well. Spread a thin layer of sauce in the bottom of a baking dish, arrange a layer of lasagne over sauce, spread a layer of ricotta and spinach mixture over lasagne, cover with a layer of sauce, sprinkle with Parmesan cheese and top with another layer of lasagne. Continue this procedure until ingredients are all used, ending with a top layer of lasagne, covered with sauce and grated cheese. Dot with butter. Bake for about 30 minutes in a preheated moderate 350° F. oven. Serve hot right from baking dish. *Serves 6 to 8.*

BAKED LASAGNE WITH TOMATOLESS MEAT AND MUSHROOM SAUCE

4 oz. dried mushrooms
¾ lb. chopped beef
2 tablespoons butter
1 tablespoon olive oil
1 small onion, minced
1 stalk celery, minced
1 tablespoon chopped
    parsley
1 small carrot, minced
3 tablespoons milk

1½ pints warm broth,
    bouillon or water
    (approximately)
salt and pepper to taste
1 lb. lasagne
¼ lb. very thin slices of
    prosciutto (or ham)
dots of butter
¼ cup melted butter
½ cup grated Parmesan
    cheese

A tempting "in Bianco" sauce (without tomatoes) enriches this lasagne dish from Piedmont.

Soak mushrooms in enough warm water to cover until softened. Drain, reserve water, and chop mushrooms coarsely. Brown meat in butter and olive oil in a saucepan with onion, celery, parsley and carrot until everything has acquired a rich color. Add the milk and mushrooms. To the mushroom water add enough broth to make 1½ pints of liquid; add to the meat and mushroom mixture. Season with salt and pepper to taste; bring to a boil, lower heat, cover and simmer for 30 minutes. Cook lasagne until tender, in rapidly boiling salted water to which

155

has been added a tablespoon of oil. Drain, rinse in cold water; drain again. Butter a rectangular baking pan and spread the bottom with a thin layer of sauce. Arrange lasagne strips in layers, side by side—3 or 4 strips to each layer. Spread each layer of lasagne with sauce and cover with slices of prosciutto, dot with butter and sprinkle with grated cheese. Repeat until ingredients are all used, ending with a layer of lasagne; pour melted butter over all and sprinkle with grated cheese. Bake in a preheated 400° F. oven for about 15 to 20 minutes or until top layer of lasagne is crisp and golden-colored. *Serves 6 to 8.*

BAKED MACARONI WITH EGGPLANT

1 lb. mezzani (short-cut macaroni)
4 quarts water, rapidly boiling, salted
2 medium-sized eggplants
½ cup olive oil
½ cup grated Parmesan cheese
3 teaspoons dried basil or 2 tablespoons chopped fresh basil

SAUCE

½ cup olive oil
1 clove garlic, whole and crushed
1 16-oz. can tomatoes
salt and pepper

Wash eggplant and peel. Cut in long thin slices. Heat olive oil in frying pan and fry slices on both sides until golden-colored and set aside. Drop macaroni in rapidly boiling water to which has been added a tablespoon of salt, and cook until almost tender. While macaroni is cooking, prepare sauce. Heat ½ cup olive oil, add garlic and brown. Remove garlic. Add tomatoes, salt and pepper to taste and let cook rapidly for a few minutes only, crushing the tomatoes with a wooden fork just a little, leaving them quite pulpy. When macaroni is done, drain and place in large mixing bowl. Drain all the oil and juice from the tomato sauce over the macaroni and add one-third of the tomatoes. (The sauce left should be rather dry and pulpy.) Mix macaroni until well blended. Butter a deep, round baking dish and cover bottom with a layer of macaroni, then a layer of fried eggplant and a generous sprinkling of grated cheese and basil, mixed well together. Repeat procedure until macaroni is all used, ending with a layer of eggplant slices. On this last layer of eggplant, which should be arranged to cover completely all the macaroni, pour the balance of the sauce, and spread evenly. Top with a generous sprinkling of the grated cheese and basil mixture, dot with butter and bake in preheated 375° F. oven for about 15 minutes. Serve right from baking dish. *Serves 4 to 6.*

BAKED MACARONI IN TWO SAUCES

1 lb. large cut macaroni	6 tablespoons grated
2 tablespoons butter	Parmesan cheese
2 tablespoons olive oil	2 tablespoons butter
2 small onions, minced	2 tablespoons flour
1 lb. ground beef	1 cup milk, hot broth,
1½ lbs. tomatoes	or stock
salt and pepper	1 egg yolk

Macaroni dressed in a meat sauce and topped with a rich Bechamel sauce makes this a luscious casserole.

Plunge tomatoes in boiling water until skins peel easily. Peel and chop. Place 2 tablespoons butter, 2 tablespoons olive oil, onions and beef in deep frying pan and brown over high heat, stirring constantly. Add tomatoes, salt and pepper and continue cooking over low heat until meat is tender, covering pan if sauce becomes too dry. When done, blend in 3 tablespoons of the grated cheese. Meanwhile cook macaroni in salted boiling water until barely tender (al dente) and drain.

Place half the macaroni in a buttered casserole or baking dish, cover with meat mixture and top with remaining macaroni. Prepare Bechamel sauce: melt 2 tablespoons butter, stir in flour, add milk and, stirring constantly, cook until it thickens. Stir in egg yolk, remove from fire, add 3 tablespoons grated cheese; blend well. Pour over macaroni and bake in preheated 350° F. oven for 30 to 45 minutes until top is nicely browned. *Serves 4 to 6.*

CANNELLONI, SICILIAN

FILLING AND SAUCE

¾ lb. chopped veal or beef
1 7½-oz. can tuna fish, chopped
1 small onion, minced
¼ lb. butter
3 tablespoons olive oil
1 cup Burgundy (red wine)
3 tablespoons tomato paste
1 tablespoon chopped parsley

pinch of thyme
½ teaspoon basil
1 egg, slightly beaten
salt and pepper
grated Parmesan cheese
butter

CANNELLONI

2 cups semolina (farina)
2 tablespoons flour
2 eggs
water

Homemade squares of dough, stuffed and rolled with a tuna fish filling that serves also as a sauce.

Filling and Sauce: Place meat and tuna fish in a saucepan with olive oil, butter and onion and brown gently over low heat for about 15 minutes. Dissolve tomato paste in wine, add parsley, pour into saucepan and mix well with rest of ingredients until smooth. Add thyme, basil and the egg. Mix and blend everything well together. Season with salt and pepper to taste. Continue cooking over low heat until sauce has thick-

158

ened, about 20 to 30 minutes. This is both filling and sauce. Meanwhile prepare cannelloni.

Cannelloni: Mix semolina and flour together well, place in a heap on work board and form a hollow in the center. Break eggs into hollow. Beat slightly with fork and combine eggs and semolina together, adding enough water gradually to form a manageable dough. Roll out very thin, dust surface with semolina, and roll up. Cut roll into strips 3 inches wide. Unroll strips and arrange one on top of the other and cut into 3-inch wide pieces, forming 3-inch squares of dough. Meanwhile bring a large pan of salted water to a rolling boil and drop squares of dough into boiling water, one at a time, to avoid sticking. Mix gently with a wooden spoon and let boil for about 15 minutes. Drain and gently pour cold water over them to prevent sticking. Arrange each square separately on a clean cloth or wax paper. Place a tablespoon or two of the filling on each square, dust with grated cheese and roll, pinching ends to hold in filling. Arrange side by side in layers in a buttered baking pan, spreading on each layer a little sauce and sprinkling with grated cheese. Dot top layer with butter and bake in a preheated hot 375° F. oven for about 20 minutes. Serve hot. *Serves 4 to 6.*

MACARONI CASSEROLE WITH SAUSAGES AND EGG TOPPING

2 tablespoons olive oil	4 or 5 quarts boiling salted water
¼ lb. butter (1 stick)	
5 Italian sweet sausages, skinned and minced	2 ounces grated Parmesan cheese
broth or bouillon	3 eggs, lightly beaten
1 lb. rigatoni	

Heat and melt ⅛ pound of butter with the olive oil in deep frying pan. When hot, add sausages and mix well, cooking slowly so sausage meat won't become dry, adding a tablespoon of broth now and then. Drop macaroni in rapidly boiling salted water and, when half-cooked, drain and place in a deep, round casserole. Place casserole over moderate flame, add the contents of frying pan and mix well. Continue cooking the macaroni by adding a tablespoon of broth now and then, as needed, until macaroni is tender and dry. This can be accomplished by cooking slowly over moderate heat, keeping the casserole covered so that, by the time macaroni is cooked, it will have absorbed the broth. When macaroni is done, add the remaining ⅛ pound of butter and the grated cheese, mixing and blending well until butter has melted. Remove casserole from heat and immediately pour beaten eggs over macaroni, mixing gently with a fork so that beaten egg will penetrate throughout macaroni. Cover pan and place over very low heat (or in a moderate oven) for a minute or two, or until eggs have set to a creamy consistency. Serve hot from casserole. *Serves 6.*

MANICOTTI

FILLING

1 lb. ricotta cheese
2 eggs
2 ounces chopped pro-
    sciutto
½ lb. mozzarella cheese,
    grated
½ cup grated Parmesan
    cheese
salt and pepper

DOUGH

3 cups flour
½ teaspoon salt
2 eggs
½ cup warm water

Filling: Blend all ingredients of filling together and set aside.

Dough: Sift flour and salt together. Place on work board, form a hollow and drop eggs in center. Beat slightly with fork and combine eggs and flour together, adding enough water gradually to form a rather stiff dough. Knead well until smooth; cover and let stand for 15 minutes. Cut in half and roll dough on floured board in 2 thin sheets. Cut into rectangles, 4 to 5 inches. Let dry for 1 hour. Cook rectangles for 10 to 12 minutes in rapidly boiling salted water. Drain, rinse with cold water and drain again. Spread a tablespoon or two of filling on each rectangle, roll and close, pressing ends together so as to prevent filling from escaping. Place filled manicotti, which resemble little muffs, side by side in a baking dish. Cover with tomato sauce (see page 188) and grated cheese. Bake in hot oven 20 to 25 minutes. Serve hot. *Serves 6 to 8.*

MACARONI IN PIQUANT SAUCE

½ cup olive oil
1 clove garlic, whole and
  crushed
1 16-oz. can tomatoes
2 tablespoons chopped
  parsley
pinch of salt
¼ teaspoon pepper

12 anchovy fillets, cut up
3 ounces capers
12 ripe olives, pitted and
  chopped
boiling broth or water
1 lb. perciatelli, linguine
  or spaghetti
grated Parmesan cheese

Heat olive oil with garlic. Remove garlic as soon as it acquires a golden tint. Add tomatoes, parsley, salt and pepper. Crush tomatoes thoroughly with a wooden fork and let cook for 2 to 3 minutes. Add anchovies, capers, olives and about ½ cup boiling broth or water. Continue cooking very slowly for about 15 minutes. Cook macaroni in boiling water, slightly salted, until tender (al dente). Drain and place in serving dish. Season generously with grated cheese, mix gently and then pour hot sauce over macaroni and mix well. Serve hot. *Serves 4 to 6.*

MACARONI POTPOURRI WITH CHICKEN LIVERS

1 lb. mezzani (short-cut
  macaroni)
10 chicken livers, cleaned
  and cut up
1 onion, chopped
1 stalk celery, chopped
2 leeks, chopped
2 small carrots, chopped

3 cabbage leaves,
  chopped
¼ cup butter
salt and pepper
1 can tomato paste, dissolved in 2 cups water
grated Parmesan cheese

Cook the macaroni in boiling salted water for about 10 minutes; drain. Brown the chopped vegetables in the butter, adding salt and pepper. When vegetables are lightly browned, add dissolved paste and continue cooking until vegetables are tender. Add livers and cook only a few minutes more. In a well-buttered casserole arrange a layer of macaroni, then spread a layer of sauce over macaroni and sprinkle generously with grated cheese, continuing until macaroni and sauce are all used, topping with sauce and cheese. Bake in preheated 350° F. oven for 25 to 30 minutes. *Serves 4 to 6.*

NEAPOLITAN RAVIOLI

DOUGH

2 cups semolina (farina)
½ teaspoon salt
2 tablespoons butter
2 cups boiling water

FILLING

½ lb. ricotta cheese
½ lb. mozzarella cheese, diced

2 eggs
2 tablespoons grated Romano or Parmesan cheese
1 teaspoon chopped basil leaf
2 teaspoons sugar
¼ teaspoon cinnamon
pinch of pepper
pinch of salt

Prepare Dough: add butter and salt to boiling water; stir over medium heat until mixture boils and butter is melted. Stir in farina gradually; continue stirring vigorously until mixture leaves the sides of pan. Remove from heat and turn onto lightly floured board; cool. Meanwhile *prepare filling:* mix all ingredients together and blend well. With well-floured hands knead dough until smooth. Roll out on well-floured board, a small piece at a time, and cut into 4- or 5-inch rounds. Place a tablespoon or two of the filling (according to size of rounds) on one-half of each round. Fold in half to form crescents. Press edges together and decorate with tines of a fork. Allow ravioli to dry for about 1 hour. Drop in rapidly boiling salted water and cook from 12 to 15 minutes. Remove carefully with slotted spoon and drain well. Serve with a favorite tomato sauce, sprinkled with a generous amount of grated cheese. Makes 18 to 24 ravioli. These are truly a treat. *Serves 4 to 6.*

RAVIOLI

Tomato Sauce (see recipe, page 188)

salt and pepper
dash of nutmeg

FILLING

1½ lbs. ricotta cheese
2 eggs, slightly beaten
¼ lb. grated Parmesan cheese
⅛ lb. mortadella, ham, prosciutto or salami, chopped (optional)

DOUGH

3 cups flour
½ teaspoon salt
2 eggs
½ cup warm water

Filling: Blend all ingredients of filling until smooth and set aside.

Dough: Sift flour and salt together. Place on board, form hollow, and drop eggs in center. Beat slightly with fork and combine eggs and flour together, gradually adding enough water to form a rather stiff dough. Knead well until smooth; cover, and let stand for 15 minutes. Cut in half and roll dough on floured board into two thin sheets. Drop tablespoonfuls of filling about 1½ inches apart on one sheet of dough, cover with other sheet. Gently press together with fingertips around each mound of filling. Cut into squares with pastry cutter. Allow ravioli to dry for one hour before cooking. Drop in 6 to 8 quarts of rapidly boiling salted water and cook 10 to 15 minutes, or until dough is tender. Remove carefully from boiling water with slotted spoon and drain well. Arrange on serving platter in layers, alternating with a layer of sauce and a sprinkling of grated cheese. Serve hot. *Serves 6 to 8.*

Meat Ravioli: Follow instructions for dough and sauce but substitute this filling: brown ½ lb. chopped beef mixed with ½ lb. chopped veal in 1 tablespoon butter with a whole clove of garlic. Remove garlic. Let meat mixture cool and mix with ½ cup chopped, cooked spinach, 1 tablespoon parsley, 2 eggs, slightly beaten, 2 tablespoons grated Parmesan cheese, and dash of nutmeg. Mix well together and proceed as above. Serve these Meat Ravioli with a rich meat sauce—see index.

MACARONI WITH SEAFOOD SAUCE

2 dozen mussels
1 dozen clams
1 tablespoon olive oil
1 lb. small squid
½ cup olive oil
1 leek, minced
1 tablespoon parsley
1 sage leaf
½ cup Chablis
2 tablespoons tomato
    paste
juice from clams and
    mussels
½ lb. fresh mushrooms,
    cleaned and sliced

2 tablespoons olive oil
salt and pepper
1 clove garlic, minced
1 lb. maccaroncelli
½ lb. shrimps, shelled and
    deveined
¼ carrot, chopped
¼ onion, chopped
1 tablespoon butter
½ cup cognac
cayenne pepper
1 tablespoon chopped
    parsley

From the seaports of Italy comes this potpourri of seafood and macaroni. A great deal of work is involved but it is well worth the trouble. Serve with it a tossed green salad, white wine and you have an exciting party dinner. To make things easier, the squid sauce may be prepared the day before (of course, heated before using) and then while the macaroni is cooking, prepare the shrimp sauce . . . Buon Appetito!

Wash clams and mussels thoroughly and place together in large deep frying pan with 1 tablespoon olive oil. Cover pan and place over high flame, shaking pan occasionally until shells open. Remove pan from heat, separate clams and mussels from shells, place in bowl and keep warm. Strain juice from clams and mussels through a fine strainer or cloth into a bowl and set aside, keeping warm. Skin the squid, cut tentacles from body, discard eyes; remove insides from body; cut body and tentacles into small pieces and wash well. Heat ½ cup olive oil in a saucepan. When hot, add leek, parsley and sage, mix and immediately add the squid, searing for a few minutes. Add the wine, mix well and let simmer until wine has almost evaporated. Add the tomato paste, mixing and blending well, then the reserved clam and mussel juice. Cover pan, lower flame and let cook very slowly until squid is tender. While these are cooking sauté mushrooms in frying pan with two tablespoons olive oil and sprinkle with salt and pepper. When liquid from mushrooms has evaporated, add garlic and continue to cook for another 2 or 3 minutes. When squid is done, add the mushrooms, clams, and mussels. Mix and blend all ingredients well together; set aside and keep warm. Cook maccaroncelli in rapidly boiling salted water until tender (al dente). While this is cooking, prepare shrimps. In small saucepan place the chopped carrot, onion and 1 tablespoon butter with shrimps and let cook slowly until shrimps are tender. Pour the cognac over shrimps, set fire to it with a match and wait until flame dies out. Turn off heat, set aside and keep warm. When maccaroncelli is cooked, drain and arrange in warm serving dish. Pour half of the sauce with squid and half of the sauce with shrimps over them, mix well, then top with the remaining squid sauce and shrimp sauce. Sprinkle with a dash of cayenne pepper and a tablespoon of chopped parsley. Serve immediately. *Serves 4 to 6.*

MACARONI TIMBALE WITH MUSHROOMS

Tomato and Chopped
Meat Sauce (see
recipe, page 184)
½ lb. lasagne (approxi-
mate)
1 lb. mezzani (small-cut
macaroni)
3 tablespoons grated
Parmesan cheese
1 lb. fresh mushrooms,
cleaned, washed,
sliced
2 tablespoons olive oil

1 clove garlic, whole
1 teaspoon parsley,
chopped

FILLING

¼ cup grated Parmesan
cheese
½ lb. mozzarella cheese,
diced
1 tablespoon butter,
melted
1 slightly beaten egg

Lasagne strips are cleverly used to enclose the filling in this festive timbale.

Cook lasagne in boiling salted water until tender. Drain, rinse in cold water and drain again, set aside. Cook macaroni in boiling salted water until almost—but not quite—tender. Drain. Place macaroni in large bowl, pour meat sauce over (reserve ½ cup of sauce), sprinkle generously with cheese and mix thoroughly.

Prepare mushrooms: while macaroni is cooking, sauté mushrooms in olive oil with parsley and garlic, mixing gently until done (about 5 minutes).

167

Prepare timbale: generously butter a 3-quart deep casserole, baking pan or ovenproof bowl and line bottom and sides with lasagne strips, starting from bottom and going up the sides, overlapping each strip a bit, with several inches overhanging the edges of casserole. Brush lasagne with melted butter. Turn into the lined casserole half of the dressed macaroni; make a hollow in center of macaroni and fill with sautéed mushrooms. Cover mushrooms and macaroni with mozzarella and top with the remaining macaroni, giving it a dome shape. Pour the reserved sauce over all. Fold over lasagne ends to cover dome completely. Brush the top with slightly-beaten egg and bake in a preheated 375° F. oven for 30 to 40 minutes. Unmold, or serve from casserole. *Serves 6.*

STUFFED DUMPLINGS BOLOGNA STYLE
FOR BROTH OR SAUCE

FILLING

2 tablespoons butter
¼ lb. loin of pork, chopped
⅛ lb. veal, chopped
⅛ lb. breast of chicken or turkey, minced
⅛ lb. prosciutto, minced
⅛ lb. mortadella, minced
salt and pepper
dash of nutmeg

2 egg yolks
2 tablespoons grated Parmesan cheese
1 or 2 tablespoons Marsala (optional)

DOUGH

3 cups flour
½ teaspoon salt
3 eggs
¼ cup warm water

These are the famous Bolognese "Tortellini" or "Cappelletti"— tiny twisted ravioli resembling little hats. Used either in broth as a soup, or boiled, strained and dressed with a rich sauce, they are highly decorative and festive. Served in the finest of Italian restaurants that feature Northern Italian cuisine.

Prepare Filling: melt and heat butter in frying pan, add pork, veal and chicken and sauté over high heat, mixing constantly for 10 to 15 minutes. Add prosciutto and mortadella and continue browning for a few minutes longer. Put mixture through food chopper, so as to obtain a smooth well-blended paste-like mixture. Season mixture with salt, pepper and nutmeg; add egg yolks and grated cheese, mixing and blending everything well, moistening if dry with a little Marsala. Cover mixture and set aside. *Prepare dough* as follows: sift flour and salt together. Place on board, form hollow and drop eggs in center. Beat slightly with fork and combine eggs and flour together, adding enough water gradually to form a rather stiff dough. Knead well until smooth; cover, and let stand for 15 minutes. Cut dough in half, then again in half and roll one-quarter at a time, keeping other quarters covered until ready to roll. Roll out very thin on well-floured board so dough will not stick. Cut into small 2″ squares or rounds 2″ across. Place ½ teaspoon filling in center of each square or round. If squares are made, fold over so as to form little triangles, press edges together and bring extreme points together, twisting and pressing together in a ring effect. If rounds are made, fold in half over filling, press edges together and bring ends together same as above. Arrange separately on a floured cloth to dry. These can be prepared a few days ahead and refrigerated until ready to use, or they can be frozen for several weeks. Serve either in chicken broth or with a sauce. *In chicken broth:* drop in boiling chicken broth (about 15 tortellini per person) and cook for about 20 minutes. Serve with grated Parmesan cheese. *With sauce:* drop in boiling salted water; cook for about 20 minutes, drain and serve dressed with Ragout Sauce, Bolognese (see page 187), and grated Parmesan cheese. *Serves 4 to 6.*

169

STUFFED DUMPLINGS FOR BROTH, TUSCAN

FILLING

1 small calf's brain
1 tablespoon butter
½ cup leftover cooked
  chicken or veal,
  chopped fine
1 slice white bread, soaked
  in a little broth and
  squeezed dry
½ cup cooked Swiss chard
  or spinach, chopped
  fine

4 tablespoons grated
  Parmesan cheese
½ lb. ricotta cheese
pinch of allspice
1 egg
salt to taste

DOUGH

3 cups flour
3 eggs
1½ quarts chicken broth

The Tuscans call these delicately stuffed little squares of dough "Agnellotti." You'll find them a festive soup course.

Filling: Parboil brain in boiling water for about five minutes. Drain and remove membrane. Heat butter in a small frying pan, add chicken or veal and sauté for a few minutes. Turn into a bowl, add brain, bread, spinach or Swiss chard, grated cheese, ricotta, allspice (no pepper) and the egg. Mix vigorously until smooth, salt to taste and set aside.

Dough: place flour on board, form a hollow well and break eggs in center; beat with fork and combine eggs and flour together, moistening with 1 or 2 tablespoons of warm water, forming a rather stiff dough. Knead for about 15 minutes until smooth. Cut dough in half and roll dough on floured board into 2 thin sheets. While rolling one-half of dough, cover other half with a towel to keep from drying. Then cover rolled sheet of dough while rolling other half. Place ½ teaspoon of filling ½ inch from the border and 1 inch apart in rows on one sheet, then cover with other sheet. Gently press together with finger tips around each dab of filling. Cut into squares (they should be quite small) with a fluted pastry cutter. Place squares, not touching each other, on a clean cloth and cover so they will not dry. Drop in boiling chicken broth and let cook for several minutes. Turn into soup tureen, serve

170

hot with a sprinkling of grated Parmesan cheese. *Serves 4 to 6.* These may also be served with a rich meat sauce, Ragout Sauce, Bolognese (see page 187). Drop in boiling salted water; cook for several minutes until tender but firm, drain and dress with the sauce and sprinkle generously with grated Parmesan cheese.

EGG NOODLES WITH BUTTER, CREAM AND CHEESE
(Fettuccine all'Alfredo)

1 lb. egg noodles	1 cup grated Parmesan
⅔ cup heavy cream	cheese (no substi-
¼ lb. soft sweet butter (1	tutes)
stick)	

This recipe has been requested time and time again; popularly known as "Fettuccine all'Alfredo," a specialty of a famous restaurant in Rome, its reputation is world-wide. "Fettucine" are homemade ⅛- or ¼-inch wide egg noodles. However, any of the fine packaged "fettucine" or egg noodles may be used. Dressing the noodles should be done with a flair and at the last moment just before serving. Restaurants use a chafing dish—and if you have one by all means use it to impress your guests. If you have no chafing dish it can all be done rather quickly and simply in a homey way by using the same pan you cooked the noodles in, a skillet or an electric skillet.

Cook the noodles in plenty of boiling salted water until tender but still firm (al dente). Drain. Melt half the butter in a chafing dish (or in the pan in which noodles were cooked) over low heat; stir in the cream and ⅓ cup grated cheese. Add the hot noodles and with a fork and spoon toss noodles gently in the butter mixture, over and over in a sort of folding process, adding the remaining butter and cheese. Mix and blend ingredients until noodles are well coated and creamy. Serve very hot with more grated cheese sprinkled over them. *Serves 4 to 6.*

Variations: Add 1 egg yolk, slightly beaten, to cream and butter mixture. For ⅔ cup cream substitute ½ cup Ricotta mixed with ¼ cup cream. Just before serving, mix in a finely slivered small white truffle.

HOMEMADE EGG NOODLES

1⅓ cups flour
2 eggs
¼ teaspoon salt, dissolved
    in a little warm water

1 or 2 teaspoons warm
    milk

Place flour on board in a mound and form a hollow in the center. Break eggs into hollow, beat eggs with a fork, adding dissolved salt. Beat and mix into the eggs the surrounding flour. When mixture becomes too stiff to work with fork, start kneading, adding a little warm milk to make it manageable and smooth. Knead dough for about 15 minutes, or until it no longer sticks to hands or the board. Dough is ready when smooth and elastic; let it stand, covered, for ½ hour. Roll out very thin and spread on a large cloth to dry, or fold dough in cloth over and over in 2- or 3-inch folds, which will prevent dough from becoming brittle. Let stand for about ½ hour,

then unfold, remove cloth and dust dough lightly with flour, gently spreading flour over the surface. Fold dough over again in 2 or 3 inch folds and slice across into ¼-inch strips. Toss strips lightly to open and separate; spread noodles out and let stand until ready to use. Cook in rapidly boiling salted water for about 10 minutes or until tender. Serve noodles with a rich meat and tomato sauce or a mushroom and sausage sauce, see Index. (For egg noodles to be used in broth, cut into ⅛-inch strips.) Noodles may be used at once or kept in a closed jar for future use. *Serves 2 to 4.*

EGG NOODLES WITH GARLIC AND BASIL SAUCE, GENOVESE (PESTO)

6 cloves garlic, minced
2 sprigs of fresh basil (about 12 leaves), minced
pinch of salt
⅔ cup grated Pecorino or Parmesan cheese
1 teaspoon butter (optional)

2 tablespoons pine nuts (optional)
½ cup olive oil
freshly ground black pepper
1 lb. egg noodles, spaghetti or linguine

This is the famous pungent Genovese green sauce, "Pesto."

This recipe requires fresh basil. If fresh basil is not available, soften ½ cup dried basil leaves in a little lukewarm water. Drain and pat dry between paper towels. The secret of a good pesto is the pounding together of the garlic and basil to a pasty consistency and the addition of the other ingredients in their proper order. It is traditional to use a mortar and pestle for this purpose. However, the same fine result can be obtained in a blender. Pound garlic and basil together until a paste is obtained; add salt; and add the cheese and olive oil alternately, a little at a time, pounding well after each addition.

173

The butter (for more flavor) and the pine nuts may be added in the same way. Stir in the pepper. Cook the egg noodles in boiling salted water until tender; drain. Dress the noodles with the sauce, tossing and mixing well. Serve with extra helpings of grated cheese. For authenticity in this Genovese recipe, one or two small potatoes, sliced very thin, are cooked in the boiling salted water until tender, before adding the pasta; when pasta is cooked, drain potatoes and pasta and dress with the sauce. *Serves 4 to 6.*

GREEN EGG NOODLES

3 cups flour	½ lb. spinach
3 eggs	pinch of salt

Cook spinach until tender. Drain thoroughly and mince or pass through food chopper. Sift flour and salt together. Place on work board, form hollow. Break eggs into hollow, beat slightly with fork, add spinach and blend with fingers, combining flour with eggs and spinach. Knead well for about 15 or 20 minutes. If necessary add a little more flour, as dough should be rather hard and smooth. Cut dough into 2 or 4 parts and roll each out, not too thin. Arrange dough sheets on clean towels to dry. When dry, but not brittle, sprinkle with flour, roll each sheet and cut into generous ¼- or ½-inch strips. Toss lightly with fingers to separate and unroll. Set aside to dry. Cook in boiling salted water for about 20 minutes or until tender. Drain. Serve with "Ragout Sauce, Bolognese" (see page 187). *Serves 4 to 6.*

SPAGHETTI WITH EGGPLANT SICILIAN STYLE

1 small eggplant, diced	1 tablespoon capers
2 roasted green peppers, cut in slivers	1 teaspoon dried basil, or 1 tablespoon minced fresh basil
½ cup olive oil	
2 cloves garlic, whole	6 anchovy fillets, cut up
1 16-oz. can tomatoes	1 lb. spaghetti
½ cup sliced pitted green or ripe olives	½ teaspoon pepper
	grated Parmesan cheese

Cut stem from eggplant, wash, dry and dice eggplant—do not peel. Roast peppers on all sides in very hot oven or under broiler, until skin is easily removed; peel, clean, and cut in slivers. Brown garlic in olive oil in saucepan or deep frying pan. Remove garlic as soon as it begins to color. Add tomatoes, crush with fork, add eggplant, and cook until eggplant is done. Add peppers, olives, capers, basil and anchovies; mix, cover and let cook for 5 or 10 minutes. When sauce is almost done, cook spaghetti in boiling salted water; drain and place in serving dish. Pour some sauce over spaghetti, sprinkle with pepper; mix gently, pour more sauce over and serve. *Serves 4 to 6.* (Serve grated cheese separately for individual taste.)

SPAGHETTI ALLA MARINARA

1 lb. spaghetti	½ teaspoon basil
⅓ cup olive oil	1 teaspoon salt
2 cloves garlic, chopped fine	pepper
½ teaspoon oregano	grated Parmesan cheese (optional)
1 16-oz. can tomatoes	
1 tablespoon chopped parsley	

175

Brown garlic in oil (do not burn), add oregano and simmer slightly, then add tomatoes, basil, parsley, salt and pepper; stir and crush tomatoes with a fork. Cook over low flame for about 15 minutes. While sauce is cooking, cook spaghetti in rapidly boiling salted water until tender; drain and place on serving dish. Pour sauce over spaghetti, mix lightly and serve. Serve with grated cheese, if desired. *Serves 4 to 6.*

SPAGHETTI WITH MEAT BALLS

SAUCE

1 1 lb. 12-oz. can
tomatoes
1 6-oz. can tomato paste,
dissolved in 1 cup of
water
1 tablespoon basil
½ teaspoon salt
dash of pepper

MEAT BALLS

1 lb. chopped beef, or ½
lb. chopped pork and
½ lb. chopped beef
1 clove garlic, chopped

2 tablespoons chopped
parsley
½ teaspoon salt
¼ teaspoon pepper
2 slices white bread
(crust removed),
soaked in milk or
water, squeezed dry
2 eggs, slightly beaten
2 tablespoons grated
Parmesan cheese
¼ cup olive oil
1 medium onion,
chopped fine
1 lb. spaghetti

Strain tomatoes into saucepan, blend in dissolved tomato paste; add basil, salt and pepper. Bring to a boil, then let simmer gently. While sauce is simmering combine meat, garlic, parsley, salt, pepper, bread, eggs, grated cheese; mix thoroughly and shape into 1- or 1½-inch balls. Heat olive oil in frying pan, add chopped onion and meatballs, browning onion and meatballs well. Be sure not to pierce meatballs while brown-

176

ing, so they will retain their juices. When onion and meatballs are well browned, pour contents of frying pan (onion, meatballs and drippings) into saucepan containing tomato sauce, and simmer together for 1½ to 2 hours. When sauce is almost ready to serve, cook spaghetti in rapidly boiling salted water until tender (al dente); drain and place on serving dish. Pour some sauce over spaghetti, mix lightly, surround with meatballs and pour more sauce over all. Serve with grated Parmesan cheese. *Serves 4 to 6.*

SPAGHETTINI WITH OIL, GARLIC AND ANCHOVY SAUCE

4 cloves garlic, minced
½ cup olive oil
1 can anchovy fillets,
    minced
1 tablespoon chopped
    parsley

1 lb. spaghettini (thin spaghetti) or vermicelli

While cooking spaghettini in rapidly boiling salted water until tender but firm (al dente), prepare the sauce. Brown garlic in hot olive oil in a small skillet until just beginning to color (discard garlic if you so desire); stir in anchovies and with a

wooden fork crush them, dissolving them slightly in the hot olive oil. Add parsley and remove from heat. Drain spaghettini and pour sauce over, toss and mix, and serve. *Serves 4 to 6.* (Anchovies may be omitted if desired, for a plain garlic and olive oil sauce.)

SPAGHETTI WITH LIGHT RED CLAM SAUCE

1 quart shelled littleneck or cherrystone clams, with their juices

⅓ cup olive oil

3 cloves garlic, cut up

pinch of oregano

1 tablespoon chopped parsley

1 tablespoon tomato paste dissolved in a little clam juice

salt and pepper to taste

1 lb. spaghetti or linguine

The Neapolitans call this light red clam sauce "Marechiaro."

Cut up clams; strain juice. In a saucepan brown garlic in hot olive oil; when browned discard garlic. Add oregano, parsley and dissolved tomato paste and simmer for half a minute. Add clam juice, bring to a boil, lower heat, cover and simmer gently for 10 minutes. Add cut-up clams, simmer for another minute and remove from heat. Meanwhile cook spaghetti in rapidly boiling salted water until tender but firm (al dente); drain. Pour sauce over spaghetti (reserve a few clams), toss, mix and top with the reserved clams. *Serves 4 to 6.* Traditionally this is served without grated cheese—but for those who desire cheese, serve it separately.

VERMICELLI CASSEROLE WITH MEATS AND VEGETABLES

1 lb. vermicelli or spaghettini	4 or 5 slices boiled tongue
3 tablespoons butter	½ 16-oz. can tomatoes, drained and slivered
Tomatoless Meat Sauce (see page 183)	1 cup peas sautéed in butter
grated Parmesan cheese	½ lb. mozzarella cheese, cut in large, thin slices
sliced breast of cooked chicken or turkey	

Cook vermicelli until tender but firm (al dente) in boiling salted water. Drain and place in a bowl; add a lump of butter, the meat sauce and grated cheese and mix thoroughly; then arrange in a round glass baking casserole, forming a dome-like shape. Decorate this dome with slices of boiled or roasted chicken breast, slices of boiled tongue, tomatoes in slivers and peas, and over all pour a little more of the meat sauce. Sprinkle with grated cheese and cover the whole with slices of mozzarella cheese. Place in a preheated 350° F. oven for 15 to 20 minutes or until mozzarella starts to melt. Serve immediately with extra helpings of sauce, served separately. *Serves 4 to 6.*

SPAGHETTI WITH WHITE CLAM SAUCE

3 dozen littleneck clams	salt and pepper to taste
1 tablespoon olive oil	¼ cup chopped fresh
¼ cup olive oil	parsley
3 cloves garlic, cut up	1 lb. spaghetti or linguine

Scrub clams clean; place in a deep skillet with 1 tablespoon olive oil. Cover tightly and cook over high heat to steam open the clams, shaking the pan frequently. When opened, remove clams from shells, strain the juice and reserve. Cut up the clams. (Or you may purchase 1 quart of littleneck clams or cherrystone clams already shelled and with their juices.) In a saucepan brown garlic in ¼ cup hot olive oil; when browned discard garlic. Add clam juice, salt and pepper to taste and boil 1 minute. Meanwhile cook spaghetti in rapidly boiling salted water until tender but firm (al dente). Just before draining spaghetti add cut-up clams and parsley to clam juice mixture and simmer for ½ minute. Drain spaghetti and pour sauce and clams over (reserve a few clams), toss, mix and top with the reserved clams. Traditionally this is served without grated cheese—but for those who desire cheese, serve it separately. *Serves 4 to 6.*

11
SAUCES

BRAISED BEEF SAUCE (TOMATOLESS)

2 to 3 lb. piece of eye round beef
5 or 6 slivers salt pork
¼ teaspoon marjoram
½ clove garlic, minced
pinch of pepper
¼ cup olive oil
2 slices prosciutto or ham minced together with 1 clove garlic and 1 tablespoon parsley
½ cup dry white wine
salt and pepper to taste
2 small onions, minced
1 carrot, minced
2 small stalks celery, minced
boiling water, broth or bouillon
1 tablespoon flour
¼ cup Marsala or sherry

What, no tomatoes? And yet this is a delicious sauce for noodles, lasagne and rice. It is particularly suited to the Vermicelli Casserole with Meats and Vegetables, see page 179. For a delicious entrée slice the meat and serve topped with sauce.

Have butcher tie meat neatly without adding any fat. Combine the marjoram, minced garlic and pinch of pepper. Rub slivers of salt pork in this mixture. Lard meat by making several incisions with thin sharp knife and insert into each cut a piece of salt pork with herb mixture, until it is all used. In heavy saucepan or Dutch oven brown meat in olive oil with prosciutto mixture, browning well on all sides. Add wine a little at a time, and allow it to evaporate. Sprinkle meat lightly with salt and pepper and continue browning to a rich deep color. Lift meat from pan and keep warm in a covered dish or bowl. Add minced vegetables to contents of pan and sauté until soft and lightly browned. Return meat to pan and brown meat and vegetables together for about five minutes, turning meat often. Then add boiling water just sufficient to cover meat. Cover pan, reduce heat and simmer gently for about 2 hours or until meat is tender. When done, remove meat to warm serving dish. Combine flour and Marsala and slowly stir into pan sauce and, stirring constantly, bring to a boil; boil gently for a minute or two, continuing to stir until sauce has thickened slightly. *Serves 4 to 6.*

CORAL COCKTAIL SAUCE FOR SEAFOOD

1 cup mayonnaise
6 tablespoons chili sauce
1 tablespoon horseradish
2 teaspoons onion juice, or 1 tablespoon grated onion

salt and pepper to taste
2 tablespoons cider vinegar
1 tablespoon lemon juice
4 tablespoons sour cream

Mix all ingredients together well until smooth. Chill and serve. Excellent for shrimp, crabmeat or lobster and as a dip.

CHOPPED MEAT AND TOMATO SAUCE, NEAPOLITAN

3 tablespoons olive oil
1 lb. ground beef, or ½ lb. ground beef and ½ lb. ground pork
1 onion, minced
2 cloves garlic, minced
1½ 6-oz. cans tomato paste dissolved in 2 cups warm water

1 16-oz. can tomatoes, strained
1 teaspoon salt
¼ teaspoon pepper
1 tablespoon chopped basil
pinch of sugar

This is the most popular of all macaroni sauces. You can substitute veal for the pork—a variety of meats makes a more richly flavored sauce. A good combination is ½ lb. beef and ¼ lb. each veal and pork. However, meat must be very lean; use top or bottom round beef, and very lean cuts for pork or veal.

Brown meat in deep saucepan in hot olive oil with onion and garlic. Add dissolved tomato paste, tomatoes, salt, pepper, basil and sugar. Cover and simmer gently for 1½ hours. This is a delicious, rich sauce for lasagne and all types of large macaroni. *Serves 4.*

MEAT AND DRIED MUSHROOM SAUCE
WITH TOMATOES AND SAUSAGES

3 lb. piece boneless chuck
   beef, rolled and tied,
   without fat
3 or 4 Italian sweet sausages
2 tablespoons olive oil
1 medium onion, minced
2 small stalks celery,
   minced
1 small carrot, minced
1 clove garlic, minced
1 tablespoon chopped
   parsley

1 teaspoon chopped basil
¼ lb. chopped beef or veal
1 Italian sweet sausage,
   skinned and crumbled
1 1 lb. 12-oz. can toma-
   toes, strained
1 6-oz. can tomato paste,
   dissolved in 1 cup
   warm water
salt and pepper
2 ounces dried mushrooms

It's a sauce—it's an entrée! A rich pot roast type of sauce, with chopped meat, perfect for a luscious lasagne casserole or any large macaroni, large egg noodles or gnocchi. Slice the meat and serve with the sausages as an entrée.

Soak mushrooms in about 1 cup warm water for one half hour. Drain, save ½ cup of the water; cut up mushrooms. In large saucepan heat olive oil and brown rolled beef and sausages. When browned remove from pan and keep warm on stove. To hot oil and drippings in pan add chopped vegetables, garlic, parsley and basil and brown. When onions are slightly colored add the chopped meat and crumbled sausage meat and sauté with vegetables for a few seconds. Add strained tomatoes, dissolved tomato paste, salt and pepper to taste, mix and blend.

Return meat and sausages to pan. Add the chopped mushrooms and ½ cup of the mushroom water. Cover and let simmer gently until sauce thickens and meat is tender, 1½ to 2 hours. *Serves 4 to 6.*

POT ROAST SAUCE WITH MUSHROOMS
FOR MACARONI

2 to 3 lb. beef (eye of round)
1 clove garlic, cut in thin slices
¼ teaspoon salt
⅛ teaspoon pepper
½ cup olive oil
1 teaspoon chopped parsley
1 medium onion, chopped
1 small carrot, chopped
1 small stalk celery, chopped
½ cup sauterne or Burgundy
1 1 lb. 12-oz. can tomatoes, strained
1 6-oz. can tomato paste, dissolved in 2 cups warm water
¼ teaspoon salt
⅛ teaspoon pepper
2 ounces dried mushrooms, or ½ lb. fresh mushrooms, sliced
1 clove (optional)

Soak dried mushrooms in a cup of warm water from ½ to 1 hour before using. Drain, save water, and chop mushrooms. Make several incisions on each side of meat and insert thin slices garlic. Tie meat, if necessary, to keep it in shape. Sprinkle meat with salt and pepper. Place oil, parsley, onion, carrot and celery in large saucepan. When oil is hot add meat and brown slowly over low flame, turning often, until meat and vegetables are all well browned. Add wine and continue cooking slowly until wine has almost evaporated. Add strained tomatoes, dissolved tomato paste, salt and pepper. Add mushrooms and mushroom water. Let sauce simmer for about 2 hours or until meat is tender. (If you prefer meat a bit rare, remove from pan just before adding tomatoes, tomato paste and mushrooms. Keep meat warm on stove and return to pan about ½ hour before sauce is cooked.) Five minutes before removing from fire, add a clove, if you wish. Pour sauce over macaroni, spaghetti or egg noodles and sprinkle with grated cheese. Slice meat and serve with sauce. *Serves 4 to 6.*

RAGOUT SAUCE, BOLOGNESE

¾ lb. beef, chopped fine
2 tablespoons butter
⅛ lb. lean unsalted pork lard, rendered, or 2 tablespoons olive oil
1 medium onion, minced
1 carrot, minced
1 stalk, celery, minced
1 clove
1 cup milk, broth or water
1 teaspoon tomato paste
salt and pepper

hot water
1 or 2 chicken livers
1 oz. dried mushrooms, soaked, drained and minced
2 small thin slices prosciutto, diced
1 teaspoon butter
¼ cup cream
1 small white truffle, sliced (optional)

This "ragu" is the famous Bolognese thick rich sauce which combines deliciously with homemade egg noodles, green noodles, gnocchi, meat ravioli or "Tortellini" (see Stuffed Dumplings, Bologna Style, page 168).

Place beef, butter, pork, onion, carrot, celery and clove in large saucepan and brown well until a deep rich color. Add milk, broth or water, ½ cup at a time (milk is traditional with this recipe and will give the sauce a fine smoothness). Add tomato paste, mix and blend thoroughly, seasoning with salt and pepper. Add just enough water to cover and let simmer very gently for about 1 hour. Meanwhile sauté in 1 teaspoon butter the chicken livers, mushrooms and prosciutto, which are then added to the sauce about 15 minutes before sauce is done. Just before serving add cream and truffle. *Serves 4.*

RAGOUT OF SAUSAGES AND MUSHROOMS

2 ounces dried mushrooms
1 carrot, chopped
1 stalk celery, chopped
1 medium onion, chopped
1 tablespoon chopped
   parsley
¼ cup olive oil

salt and pepper
pinch of nutmeg
2 Italian sausages (sweet)
2 tablespoon tomato paste,
   dissolved in 2 cups
   warm water

This is a rather thick "ragù" type of sauce—a change from the ordinary tomato sauces made with sausages. Fresh mushrooms, sliced or cut up coarsely, may be substituted for dried mushrooms, about ¼ lb. Delicious for all kinds of pasta and rice.

Soak dried mushrooms in about 1 cup warm water for ½ hour. Combine the carrot, celery, onion and parsley, and chop fine. Place olive oil in saucepan, add the vegetable mixture, nutmeg, salt and pepper, and brown for about 5 minutes over a low flame. Remove skin from sausages. Drain mushrooms. Combine sausages and mushrooms and chop. Add to vegetables in saucepan along with dissolved tomato paste. Simmer over low flame for about 1½ hours. Should it become too thick, add a little warm water. *Serves 4.*

TOMATO SAUCE, NEAPOLITAN

¼ cup olive oil
1 onion, chopped fine
1 clove garlic, minced
1 16-oz. can tomatoes,
   strained
½ 6-oz. can tomato paste,
   dissolved in ½ cup
   warm water

½ teaspoon salt
¼ teaspoon pepper
2 tablespoons chopped
   fresh basil or 2 tea-
   spoons dry basil
pinch of sugar

188

Lightly brown onion and garlic in hot olive oil. Add tomatoes, dissolved tomato paste, salt and pepper, basil and sugar. Cover and simmer gently for about 1 hour, stirring occasionally. This is a delicious basic sauce for all pasta. If a thicker, pulpy sauce is desired, do not strain the tomatoes. *Serves 4.*

"QUICK" TOMATO SAUCE

3 tablespoons butter
1 tablespoon olive oil
½ onion, minced
1 clove garlic, minced
　(optional)

1 6-oz. can tomato paste
1½ cups warm water
salt and pepper to taste
1 teaspoon dry basil (optional)

Melt and heat butter with olive oil in a saucepan, add onion and garlic and sauté until onion is soft and transparent (do not brown). (Garlic may be added, whole and crushed, and then removed when sauce is done.) Stir in tomato paste, blending well and then gradually add water, stirring constantly. Add salt and pepper to taste, and basil. Cover and simmer for 15 to 20 minutes. Use less water for a thicker sauce, if desired. This is a quick delicious sauce for all kinds of pasta, rice, meat, fish or fowl. *Makes about 2 cups.*

TUNA SAUCE FOR SPAGHETTI

2 cloves garlic, minced
¼ cup olive oil
2 tablespoons chopped
　parsley
2 7-oz. cans tuna fish

3 tablespoons tomato
　paste, dissolved in 3
　cups warm water
1 lb. spaghetti

189

Lightly brown garlic in olive oil with the parsley. Add contents of tuna cans, shredding tuna with a fork, and gently sauté for about 3 minutes. Add dissolved tomato paste, bring to a boil, lower heat and simmer for 10 to 15 minutes. (More tomato paste may be used if a richer color is desired.) Cook spaghetti to "al dente" firmness, drain and turn onto serving dish. Pour half the sauce over spaghetti, toss gently to blend, then top with remaining sauce. Can be served with or without grated cheese according to individual taste. *Serves 4 to 6.*

GREEN VINAIGRETTE SAUCE WITH ANCHOVIES

2 tablespoons chopped parsley
1 tablespoon capers, chopped
6 anchovy fillets, chopped
1 small dill pickle
1 very small boiled potato, mashed

½ teaspoon garlic juice
1 teaspoon onion juice
pinch of salt and pepper
⅓ cup olive oil
2 tablespoons vinegar

Combine and blend first 8 ingredients until a smooth mixture is obtained. Add olive oil gradually, beating with egg beater. Finish off sauce by adding vinegar. Mix and turn into serving bowl. Excellent on fish, meat or fowl. (This can be made in a blender.) *Makes about 1 cup.*

12
SALADS

STUFFED ARTICHOKE SALAD

4 globe artichokes
¼ cup vinegar
2 cups leftover cooked turkey, chicken, shrimp, lobster or crab meat
1 cup chopped celery
¼ cup minced green pepper

2 tablespoons grated onion
1 tablespoon chopped parsley
2 tablespoons olive oil
1 tablespoon vinegar or lemon juice
mayonnaise

Cut off stems and tips of artichokes. Discard some of the tough outer leaves. Wash and drain. Place artichokes upright in boiling water to which vinegar has been added and cook, covered, for about 45 minutes or until tender. Drain upside down and cool. Combine remaining ingredients, except the mayonnaise. Spread leaves of artichokes outward. Pull out tight conical center of leaves and scrape out the choke. Stuff artichokes by filling center with salad mixture. Decorate each with a generous tablespoon of mayonnaise. To eat, remove leaves one by one and dip them in mayonnaise, leaving remaining salad to be eaten with artichoke heart. Serve on bed of salad greens. *Serves 4.*

ITALIAN BEAN AND TUNA FISH SALAD

2 16-oz. cans white or red kidney beans, drained
2 tablespoons vinegar
½ teaspoon marjoram
½ teaspoon basil
1 teaspoon chopped parsley
2 stalks celery, diced

1 very small onion, minced
1 clove garlic, minced
1 7-oz. can tuna fish, shredded
2 anchovy fillets, cut up
⅓ cup olive oil
salt and pepper

Combine ingredients and let stand in salad bowl. Chill, stirring often. Serve on bed of lettuce leaves on individual plates. *Serves 4 to 6.*

CAESAR SALAD

1 cup toasted bread cubes
¼ cup olive oil
1 clove garlic, minced fine
1 cut clove garlic
2 heads romaine lettuce, washed and drained
¼ teaspoon dry mustard
¼ teaspoon freshly ground black pepper
⅛ teaspoon salt

¼ cup olive oil
1 egg
3 tablespoons wine vinegar
6 anchovy fillets, cut up
1 tablespoon capers, cut up
⅓ cup grated Parmesan cheese

Olive oil and wine vinegar are "musts" in preparing this salad; however, lemon juice may be substituted for the wine vinegar —but no substitutes for the olive oil.

Mix ¼ cup olive oil and the minced garlic, pour over toasted bread cubes and let them soak. Rub cut garlic inside salad bowl and tear lettuce into it. Mix mustard, pepper and salt in

¼ cup olive oil and pour over lettuce; toss to coat lettuce well. Break egg over lettuce and toss gently, until greens are well coated but not bruised. Add the vinegar, anchovies and capers and toss again lightly. Add the cheese and bread cubes, toss gently and serve. *Serves 4 to 6.*

CAULIFLOWER SALAD, NEAPOLITAN STYLE

1 medium cauliflower	6 anchovy fillets, cut up
3 tablespoons olive oil	1 tablespoon capers
1 tablespoon wine vinegar	12 black olives, pitted and
salt and pepper	cut into pieces

Discard leaves and stem of cauliflower; soak, head down, in salted water. Parboil in slighlty salted water for 10 to 15 minutes. Drain, rinse in cold water, and set aside until thoroughly drained and cold. Separate flowerettes. Place in salad bowl, add remaining ingredients, mix well together without breaking flowerettes. Serve on individual salad plates on a bed of salad greens. *Serves 4.*

SAVORY GREEN BEAN SALAD

1 lb. fresh green beans	1 oz. wine vinegar
1 teaspoon salt	1 clove garlic, minced
⅓ cup olive oil	crisp lettuce leaves
salt and pepper	

Wash beans, leave whole or cut in pieces on the slant. Cook in an open kettle in large amount of rapidly boiling water. Cook for 15 to 20 minutes, add salt and cook a few minutes longer. Mix and blend oil, vinegar, garlic, salt and pepper into a dressing. Drain string beans and, while still hot, pour the dressing over them, toss and refrigerate. Keep in refrigerator until ready to serve and arrange on bed of lettuce leaves. *Serves 4.*

GREEN BEAN AND STUFFED TOMATO SALAD

½ lb. fresh green beans
2 tomatoes, chilled
4 caper-stuffed anchovies
1 3½-oz. can tuna fish
⅓ cup mayonnaise

⅓ cup olive oil
2 tablespoons vinegar
crushed clove of garlic
salt and pepper to taste

Shred beans lengthwise and cook in boiling salted water until tender, about 15 minutes; drain and cool. Cut tomatoes in half crosswise, remove pulp and invert tomatoes to drain. Cream tuna fish with mayonnaise and fill the tomato cases with this mixture; top with a stuffed anchovy. Arrange green beans in the center of a serving dish lined with a bed of lettuce greens. Surround the beans with the stuffed tomatoes. Prepare a dressing with the olive oil, vinegar, garlic, salt to taste and freshly ground pepper; mix and shake thoroughly. Discard garlic and pour dressing over beans, pouring a few drops over each tomato. Chill and serve. *Serves 4.*

CONTINENTAL POTATO SALAD

3 or 4 medium-sized potatoes, cooked and diced, or sliced
½ cup chopped celery
½ cup pared, diced cucumber
½ cup chopped, pitted ripe olives

¼ cup chopped onion
¼ cup olive oil
3 tablespoons wine vinegar
1 clove garlic, crushed
salt and pepper to taste
¼ teaspoon oregano

196

Chill potatoes in refrigerator, then combine with celery, cucumber, olives and onion. Blend and mix thoroughly together the olive oil, vinegar, garlic and seasonings. Pour over potato mixture and toss lightly with two spoons. Cover and chill for an hour or two before serving. *Serves 4.*

ZUCCHINI SALAD

6 small zucchini	1 hard-cooked egg,
¼ cup chopped parsley	chopped
1 small dill pickle,	salt and pepper to taste
chopped	⅓ cup olive oil
1 tablespoon capers,	3 tablespoons vinegar
chopped	

Combine parsley, pickle, capers, egg, olive oil and vinegar; season to taste. Refrigerate. Meanwhile, cook zucchini in boiling salted water for about 10 minutes, or until just tender. Drain thoroughly; cut in quarters lengthwise or in 2-inch pieces. Turn into a bowl, pour dressing over zucchini, toss gently; chill for an hour before serving. *Serves 4.*

13
MISCELLANEOUS

CORNMEAL MUSH (POLENTA)

Bring to a rolling boil 2 quarts water with 2 teaspoons salt; add 1 lb. cornmeal (2 cups) slowly in a thin stream, stirring constantly with a wooden spoon so that no lumps are formed. Continue cooking and stirring for about 30 minutes or until cornmeal leaves sides of pan easily and is thickened. Turn onto a warm serving dish and serve hot. Chilled leftover polenta may be sliced ¼" thick and fried in olive oil; or sliced thick, toasted on both sides under the broiler and served with meat, fish or fowl. For hot cheese sandwiches: place a slice of mozzarella or any favorite cheese between two ¼" thick slices of polenta and bake or broil until cheese melts. *Serves 4 to 6.*

For a real treat try this *Baked Casserole of Polenta:* oil or butter a rectangular baking dish. Cover the bottom of dish with a good rich tomato sauce (see Index). Spread half of the polenta in dish, cover with sauce, sprinkle with grated Parmesan cheese (add sliced cooked sausages, meat or chicken for a richer dish); spread with remaining polenta and top with more sauce and grated Parmesan cheese. Bake in a preheated 350° F. oven for about 20 minutes, or until piping hot. Serve immediately.

RICOTTA GNOCCHI (Dumplings)

1 lb. ricotta cheese	salt and pepper to taste
1 cup Parmesan cheese	2 cups flour, approximately
3 eggs	

Delicious and light, these gnocchi are easy to prepare.

Drain ricotta well, pressing water from it. Beat with a wooden spoon until smooth, blend in grated Parmesan cheese and eggs; taste for seasoning. Add enough flour to make a manageable dough and knead until smooth. Form into a ball, cover and let stand from ½ to 1 hour. Cut small chunks of dough, form into finger-thick rolls and cut into 1-inch pieces. Cook a few at a time in boiling salted water, and when gnocchi come to surface (about 10 minutes) remove them with a small strainer or slotted spoon, drain well; place in layers in deep serving dish, covering each layer with generous amounts of a rich meat sauce, ragu or tomato sauce (see Index). Serve with grated Parmesan cheese for individual helpings.

Variation: add ½ cup finely chopped prosciutto or ham to dough. Instead of boiling gnocchi, roll in flour and fry a few at a time in a little butter; drain on paper and serve with a good rich sauce, or place fried gnocchi in a soup tureen or individual soup plates and pour hot broth over them. Serve with grated Parmesan cheese. *Serves 4.*

POTATO GNOCCHI (DUMPLINGS)

2½ lbs. potatoes	2 egg yolks, slightly
2 cups flour, approxi-	beaten
mately	1 teaspoon salt
	grated Parmesan cheese

Potato gnocchi are popular in Northern Italy where they are served as a first course in place of pasta. Preparing the dough while the potatoes are still warm and handling it quickly and lightly is the secret to light gnocchi that melt in your mouth.

Scrub potatoes and boil in salted water until tender but firm, about 20 minutes. Drain, peel immediately, and rub through a ricer or sieve. Place on well-floured board and mix with flour.

It is difficult to give the exact amount of flour to use. However, the mixture should be about ⅔ mashed potatoes and ⅓ flour. Make a hollow in the mixture, pour egg yolks into it, add salt; mix and knead into a soft manageable dough, handling it quickly and lightly. Cut small chunks of dough, roll quickly on well-floured board into finger-thick rolls and cut into 1-inch pieces. Press each piece with index finger making an indentation, or roll each piece on the tines of a fork, indenting with tip of finger. Arrange gnocchi on floured board or cloth and sprinkle lightly with flour to keep them from sticking together. Drop a small quantity of gnocchi into rapidly boiling salted water, stir, and when gnocchi come to surface remove with a small strainer or slotted spoon, drain well; place in deep serving dish, covering each layer with a generous amount of rich meat sauce, ragu (see Index), or melted butter, and a generous sprinkling of Parmesan cheese. *Serves 4 to 6.*

PIZZA NEAPOLITAN

For two 10-inch pies:

3½ cups sifted flour
1 envelope dry yeast
¼ cup lukewarm water
¼ teaspoon salt
1 cup lukewarm water
olive oil
1 16-oz. can tomatoes,
    drained and crushed

1 lb. mozzarella cheese,
    sliced thin
salt and pepper
2 teaspoons oregano
grated Parmesan or
    Romano cheese

Homemade pizza is a luscious treat.

Add yeast to ¼ cup lukewarm water, let stand five minutes. Dissolve salt in 1 cup lukewarm water in a bowl, add dissolved yeast and stir in 2½ cups sifted flour. Beat well to make a soft dough. Place remaining flour on board in a small heap, making a hollow in center. Place soft dough in the hollow and knead flour and dough together well until dough is smooth and elastic and does not stick to hands or unfloured board. Place dough in bowl, cover with cloth and set in warm place to rise for about 45 minutes. Punch dough down and form into two balls; knead each ball. Then place each ball in a separate bowl and cover with a cloth; set in warm place to rise again until doubled in bulk (about 2 hours). Place dough on floured board and pound lightly to deflate it. (Dough may also be purchased from bakery or prepared dough mix may be used.) Pull and stretch until each piece is large enough to cover a 10-inch lightly oiled pie pan or pizza pan, building up edges slightly. Cover with drained and crushed tomatoes; then sprinkle with salt, pepper and oregano; top with mozzarella slices, drizzle with a little olive oil and sprinkle generously with grated cheese. Bake in a preheated 400° F. oven for 30 to 40 minutes, or until mozzarella is melted and dough lightly browned and crisp. Slice pie fashion and serve hot. *Serves 4 to 6.*

Variations: arrange anchovies over tomatoes, season with pepper, add oregano and sprinkle with oil. Crisscross top of mozzarella with bacon or thin slices of cooked sausages or anchovies.

Pizza Capricciosa (Capricious)

Top with anchovy fillets, arranging them like the spokes of a cartwheel (6 in all). In the space between anchovy spokes, arrange alternately fresh chopped tomatoes, fresh chopped clams, and diced mozzarella cheese. Sprinkle with salt, pepper and oregano; drizzle with olive oil. (A little garlic powder may also be used.) Bake in a preheated 400° F. oven until ingredients are cooked, dough lightly browned and crisp, and cheese melted.

FRIED MOZZARELLA CHEESE SANDWICH

sliced white bread	1 or 2 slightly beaten eggs
mozzarella cheese	olive oil
flour	

"Mozzarella in Carrozza"—Mozzarella in a Carriage is the name given to this delicious sandwich by the Neapolitans.

Remove crust from sliced white bread. Cut mozzarella into ¼"-thick slices the size of bread slices. Place a slice of Mozzarella between two slices of bread, forming a sandwich, and press together. Dredge sandwich on both sides in flour, coating edges well, then dip in beaten egg. Set aside for a few minutes, then fry gently in hot olive oil, first on one side, then on the other. Serve immediately with lemon wedges.

Variation: add an anchovy fillet or two on top of mozzarella and proceed as above. This is called by the imaginative Italians "Mozzarella a Cavallo"—Mozzarella on Horseback!

14
DESSERTS

APPLE TORTE LAYER CAKE

3 eggs, slightly beaten
1½ cups sugar
2½ cups thinly sliced
    apples
1½ cups flour
3 teaspoons baking
    powder
½ teaspoon salt

½ teaspoon almond ex-
    tract
¾ cup chopped walnuts
1 cup heavy cream,
    whipped until stiff
2 tablespoons sugar
½ teaspoon vanilla

Blend eggs with sugar and apple slices. Sift flour, baking powder and salt together; add to apple mixture all at once and blend well. Fold in almond extract and chopped walnuts. Pour into three 8″ layer cake pans, greased and lined with waxed paper. Bake at 325° F. for 25 minutes. This makes three very thin layers. Remove from pans after running knife around edge of layers. Strip off paper. Cool and put layers together with whipped cream which has been mixed with sugar and vanilla. Decorate top layer with slices of apples topped with cream.

RUM BABA

½ cup milk
1 cake yeast
2 egg yolks
¼ cup sugar
1 whole egg
¼ cup butter, melted
½ teaspoon vanilla
2 cups sifted flour
2 tablespoons seedless
    raisins

SYRUP

½ cup sugar
¾ cup water
2 tablespoons lemon juice
2 jiggers of rum or rum
    flavoring (3 oz.)

209

Heat milk until lukewarm and dissolve the yeast in it. Beat egg yolks until thick and add sugar gradually. Beat in vigorously the whole egg. Add melted butter, while still warm, to egg mixture. Add vanilla and stir in the milk and yeast mixture. Beat in enough sifted flour, from 1¾ cups to 2 cups, to make a medium thick batter. Set batter aside, covered, in a warm place to rise for 3½ hours. Work in raisins. Butter a large ring mold, or muffin tins, and fill half full. Let batter rise again until double and bake in preheated 400° F. oven for about 25 minutes or until golden brown and cake tester comes out clean. Remove cake or cakes from pan and cool on rack.

Prepare Syrup: boil sugar and water together for about 10 minutes, add lemon juice and rum. Place cake in deep dish, pour syrup carefully over it and let marinate for several hours, basting often. Just before serving pour some additional rum over cake. Center may be filled with ice cream and topped with cherries. For individual babas, marinate in syrup as above and pour additional rum over them when serving. For added effect, place syrup-soaked babas in chafing dish, pour rum over them, heat and ignite. Serve blazing.

MY FAVORITE CHEESE CAKE

3 lbs. ricotta cheese	1 teaspoon vanilla
2 cups sugar	½ cup cream, whipped
6 egg yolks	6 egg whites, beaten stiff
½ cup sifted flour	graham cracker crumbs
grated rind of 1 lemon	

Beat ricotta until smooth, gradually adding 1½ cups sugar, then egg yolks, beating after each addition. Beat in flour, lemon rind and vanilla. Beat egg whites with ½ cup sugar. Fold whipped cream and egg whites into ricotta mixture and turn into a 12″ spring form pan which has been well buttered and sprinkled with graham cracker crumbs. Bake in a pre-

heated 425° F. oven for the first ten minutes; lower temperature to moderate 325° F. and bake for 1¼ hours. Turn off heat
and allow to cool in oven before removing. When cold, sprinkle
with confectioners' sugar and serve. Delicious also served with
a cherry glaze made as follows: drain 1 can bing cherries and
remove pits. Bring juice to boil, sugar to taste and add 2 tablespoons of cornstarch. Stirring constantly cook until thickened
and clear. Remove from stove, add cherries and cool. When
cake is cold, cover top with the thickened cherry glaze, chill
and keep refrigerated until ready to serve. Also good with a
sour cream topping: remove cake from oven when done;
spread top of hot cake with sour cream; sprinkle with toasted
slivered almonds. Return to oven, set temperature at 450° F.
and bake 8 minutes longer. *Serves 10 to 12.*

ITALIAN CHEESE CAKE WITH RAISINS

4 to 6 graham crackers	2 tablespoons lemon juice
1 tablespoon butter	1 teaspoon vanilla
2 lbs. ricotta cheese	4 eggs, unbeaten
1 cup granulated sugar	2 egg yolks
¼ cup flour	6 tablespoons raisins,
¼ teaspoon salt	soaked in rum and
2 teaspoons grated lemon	drained
rind	¼ cup heavy cream

Butter sides and bottom of 8-inch spring form pan. Roll graham crackers to fine crumbs. Coat bottom and sides of pan. Mix together sugar, flour, salt, lemon rind, lemon juice and vanilla and add to ricotta. Beat until smooth. Add eggs and egg yolks one at a time, beating after each addition. Add raisins, mix and stir in heavy cream. Turn into prepared mold. Bake 10 minutes at 400° F., then reduce temperature to 325° F., and bake 1¼ hours. Cool in oven.

Variations: Add chopped citron or chopped maraschino cherries to the filling. Top cheese cake with crushed sugared strawberries before serving. Before pouring filling into spring form, cover bottom of crumbed pan with crushed pineapple.

MOCHA CHIFFON CAKE

2¼ cups sifted flour
1 tablespoon baking powder
½ teaspoon salt
1½ cups sugar
2 tablespoons instant coffee

2 tablespoons cocoa
½ cup butter, melted
5 egg yolks
¾ cup water
8 egg whites
½ teaspoon cream of tartar

Sift together into a bowl the flour, baking powder, salt, 1 cup sugar, coffee and cocoa. Make a hollow and add the butter, egg yolks and water; beat until smooth. Add cream of tartar to egg whites and beat until soft peaks form; then add ½ cup sugar gradually and beat until stiff, glossy peaks form. Slowly pour egg mixture over meringue; gently fold until well blended. Bake in an ungreased 10-inch tube pan in a slow, moderate 325° F. oven for about 1 hour, or until the top springs back lightly when touched. Immediately turn pan upside down on a rack and let hang until cold. Loosen from sides and around tube with spatula. Turn pan over and hit edge sharply on table to loosen. If desired, spread the cake with any favorite icing.

SICILIAN CREAM CAKE (CASSATA)

2 lbs. ricotta cheese
1¼ cups sugar
½ teaspoon vanilla
1 oz. maraschino, or any
favorite white liqueur
2 tablespoons shredded
sweet chocolate, or
chocolate bits

3 tablespoons mixed
candied fruit,
chopped
sponge cake, cut in 1-
inch slices

Combine ricotta, sugar, vanilla and liqueur in a bowl and mix well with a wooden spoon until smooth and fluffy. Add chocolate, fruit, and mix well. Cut sponge cake into 1-inch slices and line bottom and sides of an 8-inch spring mold or deep pan or bowl with the cake slices. Pour ricotta mixture into lined mold. Cover top with cake slices and place in refrigerator overnight or in freezer for several hours. If in pan or bowl, invert onto serving dish and sprinkle top with confectioners' sugar. If using spring mold, remove spring rim, place cake on serving plate with bottom tin and sprinkle top with confectioners' sugar.

ORANGE RUM RING CAKE

2⅔ cups sifted flour
2½ teaspoons baking
powder
½ teaspoon salt
¼ teaspoon baking soda
pinch of powdered ginger
⅔ cup butter
1⅓ cups sugar
3 egg yolks

1½ teaspoons grated
orange rind
½ cup unstrained orange
juice
½ cup rum
½ teaspoon each almond
and vanilla extracts
3 stiffly beaten egg whites

213

Sift first five ingredients together twice. Cream butter until fluffy and light, gradually add sugar, creaming well. Add egg yolks, one at a time, beating well after each addition, then add orange rind. Gradually add dry ingredients alternately with orange juice mixed with rum. Beat well and stir in extracts. Fold in egg whites. Pour batter into a buttered 9-inch tube cake pan and bake in a moderate 350° F. oven for 45 to 60 minutes, or until firm. Serve sprinkled with confectioners' sugar, or top with a favorite icing.

PANETTONE (SWEET RAISIN BREAD, MILANESE)

3 cakes yeast, or 3 en-
velopes
¼ cup lukewarm water
½ cup lukewarm milk
½ cup flour
4 cups sifted cake flour
½ cup sweet butter
⅓ cup sugar, sifted

3 egg yolks
2 whole eggs
¼ teaspoon salt
1 teaspoon grated lemon
rind
⅔ cup seedless raisins
¼ cup small thin slivers
of citron

An 8-inch round pan, at least 7 or 8 inches deep, is required to bake this sweet bread. To make pan deep cut a double thickness of aluminum foil 8 inches wide and long enough to go around the pan like a collar with ends overlapping. Fasten ends at top and bottom with paper clips or pins and tie collar around pan. Grease pan and inside of collar.

Dissolve yeast in lukewarm water, add milk and stir in ½ cup flour; cover with a cloth and let rise in warm place for 1 hour. Cream butter until soft, add sugar gradually and beat until light and creamy. Beat in egg yolks and whole eggs, beating after each addition; add salt and lemon rind. (If salt butter is used, omit salt.) Add yeast sponge and 4 cups flour to make a soft dough. Turn on lightly floured board and knead until smooth and elastic. Place in a greased bowl; brush top

214

with a little melted butter. Cover and let rise in a warm place for 2 to 3 hours or until dough has doubled in bulk. Punch down and turn onto a lightly floured board, knead a little, then knead into it raisins and citron. Shape dough into a ball and place in prepared greased pan. Cut a deep cross on top. Cover with a cloth and let rise until doubled in bulk, about 1½ to 2 hours. Brush with melted butter and bake in a preheated 400° F. oven for 10 minutes, lower heat to 350° F. and bake for 45 minutes or until cake tester comes out clean and cake is brown, brushing with butter once more while baking.

FRENCH PEACH CAKE

2½ cups sliced fresh
    peaches
⅓ cup sugar
cinnamon or nutmeg
grated rind of 1 lemon
juice of 1 lemon
1 well-beaten egg
2 tablespoons butter,
    diced

BATTER

1 cup sifted flour
½ cup sugar

1 teaspoon baking powder
¼ teaspoon salt
2 egg yolks, beaten
1 tablespoon melted butter
½ cup milk

MERINGUE

2 egg whites
pinch of salt
¼ teaspoon cream of tartar
4 tablespoons sugar
½ teaspoon vanilla extract

Grease a deep 8" pie pan or ovenproof dish. Cover bottom well with sliced peaches. Sprinkle fruit with sugar, cinnamon or nutmeg, lemon rind and juice. Cover with well-beaten egg and dot with butter. *Prepare Batter:* sift flour again with sugar, baking powder and salt. Add egg yolks, butter and milk. Beat these ingredients with swift strokes until they are blended. Cover fruit with the batter. Bake in a preheated, hot 425° F. oven for about 30 minutes. Turn out cake on an ovenproof platter, peach side up. Cool slightly. Whip the two egg whites with a pinch of salt and ¼ teaspoon cream of tartar until they stand in peaks, then beat in 4 tablespoons granulated sugar and ½ teaspoon vanilla. Cover cake with this meringue and bake in a slow 300° F. oven for 15 to 20 minutes.

ITALIAN RUM CAKE

ZABAGLIONE CREAM

6 egg yolks
5 tablespoons sugar or honey
¾ cup Marsala or sherry

¼ teaspoon vanilla, grated lemon or orange rind
8″ spongecake
⅓ cup rum
1 cup heavy cream, whipped

Prepare Cream: beat eggs with sugar in top of double boiler until thick. Place over hot water and add wine gradually, beating constantly until the consistency of heavy cream. Do

not allow to boil; fold in flavoring. Remove from heat at first sign of bubble. Cut spongecake into 3 layers. Place bottom layer on cake plate, brush surface with rum and spread half of the Zabaglione cream over it. Top with second layer; brush with rum and spread with remaining cream. Cover with third layer. Refrigerate. When ready to serve, cover top and sides of cake with whipped cream.

FRUIT SAVARIN

1 cup mixed diced glazed fruit
Cointreau, rum or brandy
½ cup milk, scalded
1 cake yeast
6 egg yolks
½ cup sugar

¼ cup warm melted butter
1 teaspoon vanilla
1¾ cups sifted flour (approximately)
½ cup sugar
½ cup water

Place fruit in a small bowl, cover with liquor and let stand. Cool milk to lukewarm and dissolve in it the yeast. Beat egg yolks until thick and add sugar gradually. Add melted butter while still warm to egg mixture. Add vanilla and stir in the yeast mixture. Beat in enough flour to make a medium-thick batter. Set batter aside, covered, in a warm place to rise for about 3½ hours. Then drain fruit, reserve liquor, and stir drained fruit into batter. Spoon batter into a buttered fluted ring mold. Cover and let rise again until doubled in bulk and then bake in a preheated 350° F. oven for 25 to 30 minutes or until golden brown and the cake tester comes out clean. Meanwhile, prepare syrup: combine ½ cup sugar and ½ cup water and boil for about 10 minutes, remove from heat, stir in reserved liquor. When cake is done remove from oven, let stand a few minutes, then unmold in a deep dish. While cake is still warm spoon the syrup carefully all over it. Let cool and serve. Good, also, served warm.

SAVOY RING CAKE

8 egg yolks
1½ cups sugar
1 teaspoon vanilla
1 cup sifted cake flour

½ teaspoon salt
8 egg whites, beaten stiff
confectioners' sugar

Beat egg yolks until light, add sugar and beat together for about 15 minutes. Add vanilla and cake flour, resifted with salt. Beat until well blended. Fold in egg whites carefully. Pour into a well-buttered ring pan and bake in moderate 350° F. oven for 1½ hours, or until cake shrinks from sides of pan. Serve dusted with confectioners' sugar.

ITALIAN SPICE CAKE

1½ cups boiling water
¾ cup honey
1⅛ cups sugar
2½ teaspoons baking soda
pinch of salt
3 tablespoons rum
1 teaspoon Anisette
     Liqueur

1 teaspoon cinnamon
4 cups sifted flour
4 tablespoons chopped
     blanched almonds
2 tablespoons chopped
     citron
1 teaspoon grated orange
     rind

Stir together the first 5 ingredients until sugar is dissolved. Stir in rum, Anisette and cinnamon, mixing well. Stir slowly into flour and beat to form a smooth batter. Add the almonds, citron and orange rind. Turn into a buttered loaf pan and bake in preheated hot 450° F. oven for 10 minutes; reduce heat to moderate 375° F. and bake for about an hour longer or until cake tester comes out clean. Cool and unmold. Slice thin and serve with sweet butter and honey. This is even more delicious the second day.

ANISE BISCUITS

2 eggs
⅝ cup sugar
1¼ cups cake-flour * sifted

1 teaspoon anise seeds
1 egg white, beaten stiffly
butter

Place eggs and sugar in bowl and beat well 10 minutes. Add flour slowly, blending gently and thoroughly. Add anise seeds and fold in stiffly-beaten egg white. Butter and flour a loaf pan 4 inches wide. Place batter in pan and bake in moderate oven (375° F.) 20 minutes. Remove from pan, leaving oven turned on, cut loaf into ½-inch slices and place these on buttered cookie sheet. Again place in oven. Brown slices first on one side and then on the other. *Makes 16 to 18 biscuits.*

FLORENTINE COOKIES

½ cup cream
3 tablespoons butter
½ cup sugar
1 tablespoon rum
1¼ cups finely chopped
   almonds

⅓ cup sifted flour
¾ cup finely chopped
   candied orange peel
melted chocolate

Combine cream, butter and sugar in a saucepan and gently bring to a boil. Remove from heat and stir in rest of ingredients, except chocolate. If batter is too thin, add a little more flour. Drop batter by tablespoonfuls onto well-greased baking sheet, about three inches apart. Bake at 300° F. for 10 to 15 minutes. Cool for about 5 minutes and remove immediately with a spatula to a rack. Spread tops with melted sweet or bitter chocolate and let set. *Makes about 24 cookies, depending upon size.*

---

* If all-purpose flour is used, remove 2 tablespoons from each cup of flour and add, instead, 1½ tablespoons of cornstarch.

ITALIAN MACAROONS

½ lb. almonds, blanched
1 cup sugar
2 egg whites, beaten
  stiffly

½ teaspoon almond ex-
  tract (optional)
confectioners' sugar

Chop almonds very fine, almost to a powder. Add sugar, mix well and add egg whites. Add almond extract and blend all together gently but thoroughly. Butter and flour a baking sheet and drop almond mixture on the sheet by teaspoonfuls, shaping and rounding with blade of knife. Sprinkle with confectioners' sugar and let stand for an hour or two. Bake in moderate oven 375° F. for about 5 minutes, or until delicately brown in color. *Makes about 20 macaroons.*

PINE NUT COOKIES

1½ cups sugar
4 eggs
grated rind of half a lemon

2 cups cake flour
confectioners' sugar
pine nuts

Break eggs in top of double boiler, add sugar, place over hot water and beat gently until egg mixture is warm. Do not overheat as this would cook the eggs and spoil the mixture. When mixture is warm, remove from heat and continue beating until eggs are foamy and cooled. Add lemon rind and very slowly and gradually add the flour, folding and mixing gently so as not to spoil the eggs' frothiness. Drop by teaspoonfuls on buttered and floured baking sheet, or use a cookie or pastry bag, shape into circles and leave a 1" space between them. Cover each with pine nuts, sprinkle confectioners' sugar over them and let stand for about 10 minutes. Bake in 375° F. oven for about 15 minutes or until golden colored. *Makes about 40 cookies.*

QUEEN'S BISCUITS (SESAME COOKIES)

½ cup sugar
½ cup softened butter
1 egg
¼ to ⅓ cup of milk
1 teaspoon orange extract
1 teaspoon vanilla

2½ cups flour, sifted
¼ teaspoon salt
1 tablespoon baking powder
sesame seeds

Cream butter and sugar well together, beat in egg. Gradually add milk and flavoring, beating well. Sift flour, baking powder and salt together and add to creamed mixture, mixing together to make a soft manageable dough (if too dry, add a little more milk). With floured hands roll into a ball; wrap in wax paper and chill for an hour or two. When ready to prepare cookies, spread sesame seeds on wax paper; break off pieces of dough the size of a small walnut and roll in sesame seeds. Arrange on an ungreased cookie sheet about an inch apart and with the back of a tablespoon flatten out into ¼-inch rounds. Bake in hot 425° F. oven for 12 to 15 minutes or until golden brown. With spatula remove from cookie sheet and cool on rack. *Makes 2 to 3 dozen cookies.*

ITALIAN CREPES FLAMBÉ

CREPES

1 cup flour
4 eggs
pinch of salt
1 tablespoon sugar
2 tablespoons butter,
   softened
grated rind of 1 lemon
grated rind of 1 orange
1 cup milk

butter
12-oz. jar favorite jam or
   marmalade
1 tablespoon sugar
2 or 3 tablespoons water
3 jiggers cognac or
   brandy (4½ oz.)
2 or 3 lumps sugar

Prepare Crêpes: combine first 7 ingredients and beat, gradually adding the milk. Melt a little butter, just enough to grease the bottom of a 6″ or 8″ skillet, pour 2 or 3 tablespoons of batter into the skillet, or enough to cover bottom of pan, tilt pan back and forth to spread evenly. Brown on one side, then the other. As each pancake is done, set aside and keep warm. Repeat until all batter is used. Place jam in a small saucepan with 1 tablespoon sugar and water, bring to a boil; stir in 1 jigger of cognac and blend well. Arrange warm crêpes in a stack in serving dish or chafing dish, spreading each pancake with a little of the jam mixture. Pour remaining mixture over all. Meanwhile soak sugar lumps in remaining cognac and place sugar on top of crêpes; pour over cognac and set a flame to it. Serve cut in wedges, pie fashion. A combination of Cointreau and cognac may be used—and the amount of the liquor is according to your taste!

RICE FRITTERS, FLORENTINE

2 cups cooked moist rice
3 beaten eggs
½ cup sugar
½ teaspoon vanilla
1 tablespoon lemon rind, grated
½ cup seedless raisins (optional)

1 tablespoon rum
3½ teaspoons baking powder
6½ tablespoons flour
hot fat for deep frying
confectioners' sugar

Soak raisins in warm water until they swell; drain thoroughly. Combine rice with the next 8 ingredients, mixing and blending well. Drop batter into hot fat by teaspoonfuls and fry until fritters are a golden brown. Drain on absorbent paper. Serve sprinkled with confectioners' sugar.

SPUMONE

MIXTURE NO. 1

2 cups milk
2 tablespoons cornstarch
5 egg yolks

¾ cup sugar
1 teaspoon vanilla
2 tablespoons chopped nut meats

Combine ingredients in a saucepan by blending the cornstarch first in ½ cup cold milk and then adding balance of milk, sugar, egg yolks and vanilla. Cook over low flame, stirring constantly, until thick. Do not boil. Cool; fold in nutmeats and freeze partially, so that mixture is soft enough to be spooned out easily.

MIXTURE NO. 2

1 cup heavy cream
½ cup confectioners' sugar
10 maraschino cherries, cut in small pieces

2 tablespoons finely chopped candied fruit mix
10 blanched almonds, cut in slivers

223

Whip cream until frothy, gradually add sugar and whip until stiff. Gently fold in cherries, candied fruit mix and almonds. Chill thoroughly in refrigerator. A large aluminum melon-shaped mold is usually used. Individual aluminum molds can also be used. Chill molds thoroughly before using. When mixture no. 1 is ready line inside of mold with ⅔ of this partially frozen custard, packing it in with back of spoon or spatula, leaving a hollow in center. Fill hollow quickly with mixture no. 2 and then cover and pack well with remaining mixture no. 1, spreading evenly. Cover top of mold with aluminum foil and freeze for several hours. When ready to serve dip mold briefly in warm water and unmold. For added zest serve with a dash of apricot brandy or Cointreau.

STRAWBERRY FRITTERS

1 pint large fresh straw-
berries
2 cups crumbled maca-
roons or graham
crackers
½ cup orange marmalade,
or any desired jelly or
preserve

BATTER

1 egg
¾ cup milk
1 tablespoon sherry,
brandy, rum or lemon
juice
1 cup sifted flour
1 teaspoon baking powder
¼ teaspoon salt

Wash, hull and drain strawberries. Coat strawberries with a thin layer of marmalade (if marmalade is too thick, thin with a little sherry or rum) and then roll in crumbs until well coated; set aside to dry.

Prepare Batter: sift flour, baking powder and salt together. Beat egg and milk together, add liquor and stir in dry ingredients, mixing until a smooth batter is obtained. Dip each strawberry into the batter and fry in deep hot fat until lightly brown and puffy. Drain on paper. Sprinkle with confectioners' sugar or roll in granulated sugar.

ZABAIONE or ZABAGLIONE

6 egg yolks
5 tablespoons sugar or
    honey
¾ cup Marsala or sherry

¼ teaspoon vanilla, grated
    lemon or orange rind
    (optional)

A foamy egg dessert served hot in tall glasses—a nectarlike concoction. If a portable electric beater is used it will take only a few minutes—do not allow mixture to come to a boil and when the right consistency is attained, spoon immediately into the tall glasses and serve.

Beat eggs with sugar or honey in top of double boiler until thick. Place over hot water and add wine gradually, beating constantly until thick and foamy and the consistency of whippped cream. Do not allow to boil. Remove immediately from heat at first sign of bubble. Spoon into parfait glasses. It can also be served cold. This foamy cream can also be served over well-chilled berries, puddings, slices of cake or biscuits. *Serves 4.*

ZUPPA INGLESE

1 lb. ladyfingers, sepa-
    rated
1 to 1½ cups rum

VANILLA OR PASTRY CREAM

3 egg yolks
3 tablespoons sugar

3 tablespoons flour
pinch of salt
2 cups milk
rind of 1 lemon
½ teaspoon vanilla

Zuppa Inglese, literally translated, means "English soup." It is a delicate, creamy dessert, layered with ladyfingers soaked in rum. This recipe dates back to the end of the Eighteenth Century. A romantic legend would have us believe that it was concocted by the royal chefs of Naples in honor of Lord Nelson and Lady Hamilton when the King and Queen of Naples were restored to their capital, through the efforts of Lord Nelson and his "inamorata."

Prepare Cream: beat egg yolks and sugar well together in a saucepan and, beating constantly, gradually add flour, a tiny pinch of salt, then the milk a little at a time. Add lemon rind, place over moderate heat and, stirring constantly with a wooden spoon, let cook until mixture reaches boiling point and has thickened. Do not boil. Remove from fire, remove lemon rind and let cool. Stir occasionally to prevent skin from forming over top. Line bottom of a deep 10- or 12-inch plate or cake pan with separated ladyfingers, each generously brushed with rum, spread cream thickly over them, then another layer of ladyfingers and another layer of cream. Repeat until cream and ladyfingers are all used, ending with a thick layer of cream. Refrigerate to chill and set. Serve as is, or topped with whipped cream and sprinkled with chopped candied cherries, or top with meringue made with the remaining 3 egg whites, beaten with 4 tablespoons of sugar. In the latter case, pile the meringue on cake and bake in moderate 350° F. oven for several minutes until meringue is lightly colored. Cool and refrigerate to serve cold.

BRIOCHE

½ cup milk
½ cup butter
⅓ cup sugar
½ teaspoon salt
¼ cup warm water
1 package dry or cake
    yeast

1 egg yolk, beaten
3 eggs, beaten
3¼ cups sifted flour
1 egg white
1 tablespoon sugar

Scald milk. Cool to lukewarm. Cream butter. Gradually cream in sugar and salt. Measure water into a mixing bowl. Sprinkle or crumble in yeast; stir until dissolved. Stir in lukewarm milk and creamed mixture. Add egg yolk, eggs and flour. Beat 10 minutes. Cover and let rise in a warm place, free from draft, until doubled in bulk. Stir down and beat thoroughly. Cover tightly with waxed paper or aluminum foil. Store in refrigerator overnight. Punch down and turn out soft dough on floured board. Divide into two parts, one about ¾ of dough and the other about ¼ of dough. Cut larger part into 16 equal pieces. Form into smooth balls and place in well-greased muffin pans. Cut smaller part of dough into 16 equal pieces and form into smooth balls. Make a deep indentation in center of each large ball and dampen slightly with cold water. Press a small ball into each depression. Cover and let rise in a warm place, free from draft, about 1 hour or until more than doubled in bulk. Brush with mixture of egg white and 1 tablespoon sugar. Bake in preheated 375° F. oven about 20 minutes.

CANNOLI ALLA SICILIANA

SHELLS

2 cups flour
2 tablespoons shortening
1 teaspoon sugar
¼ teaspoon salt
about ¾ cup Marsala,
    Burgundy, or Chablis
vegetable oil for deep frying
1 egg white

FILLING

1½ lbs. ricotta cheese, well
    drained

½ lb. confectioners' sugar
¼ teaspoon cinnamon
½ square unsweetened
    chocolate, grated, or
    ½ tablespoon cocoa
vanilla
6 tablespoons chopped
    citron peel
3 tablespoons chopped
    candied orange peel
6 glazed cherries, halved

To make cannoli shells it is necessary to have 3 or 4 metal tubes, made preferably from very lightweight tin, about 7 inches long and 1⅛ inches in diameter. The edges should be brought together and not soldered. (A local tinsmith will be glad to make these for you.) Bamboo tubes or a broomstick cut to size are also used, but for sanitary reasons metal tubes are best. The initial cost is very little and once made they will serve indefinitely. These can now be found in the housewares department of many department stores.

Shells: combine the flour, shortening, sugar and salt, and gradually add wine, kneading together until a rather hard dough is formed. Form into a ball, cover with a cloth and let stand for about 1 hour. Cut dough in half, roll and stretch one half of dough into a thin sheet about ⅛ inch thick, or less, and cut into 4-inch squares. Place a metal tube diagonally across each square, from one corner to another; wrap dough around tube by overlapping the other two corners, sealing the overlapping dough with a little egg white. Heat oil meanwhile in large deep pan for deep frying. Drop one or two of the tubes at a time into the hot oil, fry gently on all sides until dough acquires a golden-brown color. Remove from pan, let cool a little, gently remove shell from metal tube. Set shells aside to become cold. Repeat procedure until shells are all made. *Makes about 10 to 12 shells.*

Filling: mix ricotta thoroughly with dry ingredients: confectioners' sugar, cocoa and cinnamon (chocolate or cocoa may be omitted entirely). Add a drop or two of vanilla flavoring, chopped fruit peel. Mix and blend well. A little grated pistachio may be added if desired. Chill mixture thoroughly in refrigerator before filling shells. Fill cold cannoli shells and smooth, filling evenly at each end of shell. Decorate each end with a piece of glazed cherry, sprinkle shell with confectioners' sugar. Refrigerate until ready to serve.

CREAM PUFFS

Pastry Cream

3 tablespoons powdered
    sugar
3 egg yolks
3 tablespoons cake flour
strip of lemon peel
¼ teaspoon vanilla
1 pint milk
1 teaspoon butter

Puffs

½ cup shortening
⅛ teaspoon salt
1 cup boiling water
1 cup sifted flour
3 eggs

Prepare Cream: place sugar and egg yolks in a saucepan and mix with a wooden spoon; add flour gradually. Add lemon peel and vanilla. Heat milk almost to the boiling point and pour a little at a time into above mixture, beating mixture constantly with a wooden spoon; let thicken and bring to a boil. Boil gently for about 4 or 5 minutes. Remove from heat, add butter, mix and blend and turn into a bowl to cool, stirring now and then.

Prepare Puffs: Add shortening and salt to boiling water and stir over medium heat until mixture boils. Lower heat, add flour all at once and stir vigorously until mixture leaves the sides of pan. Remove from heat and add 1 egg at a time, beating thoroughly after each addition. Shape on an ungreased cookie sheet using 1 teaspoon or 1 tablespoon of paste for each puff (depending upon size desired). A pastry bag may be used. Bake in hot 450° F. oven for 20 minutes; reduce temperature to moderate 350° F. and bake about 20 minutes longer. Remove from oven and cool on rack. When puffs are cold, slit open at top and fill with pastry cream.

Variations: puffs may be filled with whipped cream, sweetened and flavored with vanilla; a combination of strawberries and whipped cream; or ricotta cream prepared as follows: combine 1 cup ricotta cheese with ¼ cup confectioners' sugar and ½ teaspoon vanilla; mix until smooth.

229

EASTER CREAM PUFF DESSERT
(Dolce di Beignets)

Puffs (Beignets) (See
page 229)

CHOCOLATE CHEESE
CREAM

1 cup sugar

1½ lbs. ricotta cheese
3 tablespoons cocoa
1 tablespoon rum

Prepare puffs according to instructions, using 1 teaspoon of paste mixture for each puff. When puffs are cold make a small opening in the bottom of each, gently fill with chocolate cheese cream and arrange bottom side down in a round cake dish, side by side in circles. Cover cream puffs with the remaining chocolate cheese cream, garnish all around edge with whipped cream and top with shaved chocolate or tiny chocolate bits.

Chocolate Cheese Cream: mix sugar and ricotta thoroughly. Add cocoa and rum. Blend until mixture is of custard-like consistency. Chill.

HONEY BALLS or BUBBLES (STRUFFOLI)

3 cups sifted flour (ap-
    proximately)
4 eggs
1 egg yolk
¼ cup soft lard or short-
    ening
1 tablespoon sugar
¼ teaspoon salt
1 tablespoon grated lemon
    peel

hot fat for deep frying
1½ to 2 cups honey
2 tablespoons grated
    orange rind
½ cup citron, finely
    chopped
Multi-colored sprinkles

Struffoli—a Neapolitan Christmas sweet, all honey and golden colored, covered with myriads of multi-colored sprinkles.

Place 2½ cups of flour into a bowl, form a hollow in the center and break into it 4 eggs; add the egg yolk, lard, sugar and salt. With a wooden spoon work ingredients together, then with the hands, until dough cleans the bowl, adding another ½ cup of flour if necessary. Knead on a lightly floured board until dough is smooth and does not stick to fingers. Cut small pieces from dough; roll into long narrow ropes and cut into ⅛" or ¼" pieces. Roll each piece between palms into tiny balls. Fry a handful at a time in deep hot fat until golden brown.

231

Remove from hot fat with slotted spoon and drain on paper. Melt honey in a large saucepan over moderate heat, add the "Struffoli" and gently stir with a wooden spoon, so as not to crush the "bubbles," adding grated orange rind and citron. Stir very gently until "Struffoli" have thoroughly absorbed the honey. Turn onto a serving platter in a mound and with wet hands shape into a cone. Cover with multi-colored sprinkles, cool and serve.

"PASTICIOTTI," A NEAPOLITAN PASTRY

PASTRY (Pasta Frolla)

2 cups sifted all-purpose
    flour
pinch of salt
½ cup butter, cut into
    small pieces
½ cup sugar
2 egg yolks
grated rind of 1 lemon

FILLING

1½ lbs. ricotta cheese
6 tablespoons confec-
    tioners' sugar
2 egg yolks
pinch of cinnamon
1 teaspoon grated lemon
    rind
4 tablespoons raisins (op-
    tional)

Prepare Pastry: sift flour, salt and sugar into a bowl. Cut in butter with a pastry blender or with finger tips, to distribute the butter evenly through the flour. Add egg yolks, one at a time, mixing with a wooden spoon after each addition; blend in lemon rind. Work with hands until dough is soft and manageable and cleans the bowl, adding a little water if necessary to hold together. Turn onto a board and knead quickly until smooth. Wrap in wax paper and refrigerate for an hour or two. Roll out, on a lightly floured board, about ¼" thick. Cut pastry into rounds about 1" larger than diameter of muffin cups, grease the cups and fit pastry rounds smoothly into them.

Filling: combine ricotta with rest of ingredients, mix and blend well with wooden spoon. Fill prepared pastry cups. Cut left-over pastry into small strips and place strips crisscross over filling; trim edges. Bake in moderate 350° F. oven for 40 to 50 minutes. Cool in oven. *Makes eight to ten pastries.*

RIBBONS AND BOWS

1 tablespoon butter	1 tablespoon cognac
2 tablespoons sugar	pinch of salt
2 eggs, beaten	milk
drop of vanilla	deep fat for frying
1½ cups flour	

These are the delicious fluffy-fried pastry strips that are served with the coffee in fine Italian restaurants. The imaginative Italians give them many names: Nastrini (tiny ribbons); Chiacchiere (tittle-tattle); Cenci (rags); Bugie (lies); Lingue delle Suocere (tongues of mothers-in-law)!!

Cream butter and sugar together in a bowl, add eggs, mix thoroughly. Add vanilla. Gradually add 1 cup of flour, the cognac, and salt, beating constantly. Place ½ cup of flour on work board in a heap, form a hollow in center, turn mixture

into it and, kneading well, combine flour and mixture together to obtain a smooth, not too hard dough. If dough becomes hard in kneading, soften with a little milk. Form into a ball, cover with a clean cloth and let stand for about 10 to 15 minutes. Roll out into a large sheet, ¼ inch thick. Cut with fluted pastry cutter in ribbon strips ½ to 1 inch wide and 6 inches long. Form into bows or any other shape desired and fry a few at a time in deep, hot fat until crisp and golden brown. Remove from fat as done and drain on paper. Sprinkle immediately with confectioners' sugar.

RICOTTA CHEESE TARTLETS (CASSATINE)

TART PASTRY

2 cups sifted flour
2 tablespoons sugar
2 egg yolks
½ cup butter
water

FILLING

1 tablespoon flour
1 tablespoon confectioners' sugar

1 egg yolk
½ cup boiling milk
½ cup cold milk
3 tablespoons butter
½ lb. ricotta cheese
2 tablespoons confectioners' sugar
1 jigger rum (1½ oz.)
½ teaspoon vanilla
candied cherries

Tarts: place first 4 ingredients in a bowl; mix by hand until butter is broken into fine particles. Add just enough water to hold mixture together. Chill thoroughly and roll out about ¼ inch thick. Cut into rounds, fit into tart pans and prick well with a fork, or fit over back of muffin tins by fitting dough tightly around tins, pleating it at regular intervals and pricking well with a fork. Bake in a very hot 450° F. oven for 12 to 15 minutes, or until delicately browned.

Filling: mix and blend with a wooden spoon the flour, confectioners' sugar and ½ cup cold milk; stir in egg yolk. Place over moderate heat and gradually add ½ cup boiling milk, stirring constantly; cook until smooth and thickened. Remove from heat and cool. Cream butter, add ricotta and beat until blended. Blend into this mixture, a little at a time, the cooled custard, then the 2 tablespoons confectioners' sugar, rum and vanilla. Beat lightly until well blended. Fill tart shells, spreading evenly on top; decorate each with a halved candied cherry. Chill until set and serve.

FRUIT ROLL PIE

SWEET PASTRY

1 cup sifted flour
1 teaspoon baking powder
1 tablespoon sugar
¼ cup butter
1 egg, lightly beaten
sherry or cognac

FILLING

orange marmalade
5 or 6 apples, peeled and
    cut into very thin
    slices
¼ cup seedless raisins
½ cup sugar
¼ teaspoon cinnamon

Combine flour, baking powder and sugar. Cut in butter with 2 knives or pastry blender, add egg and mix thoroughly, moistening with sherry to hold together. Knead lightly and roll out into an 8 x 16 inch rectangle, about ¼ inch thick. Place on an ungreased jelly roll pan. Mix apples, raisins, sugar and cinnamon together. Spread entire surface of dough with marmalade and top one half of the length of the dough with the apple mixture. Fold the other half of dough over carefully to cover apples. Press top dough down lightly; curve into a slight crescent shape. Cut gashes in top every 2 inches. Brush surface lightly with milk and sprinkle with a combination of sugar and cinnamon. Bake in a preheated 350° F. oven for about 40 minutes. Cool, slice and serve.

PUMPKIN CHEESE PIE

Sweet Pastry	Filling
2 cups sifted flour	⅛ teaspoon salt
1 teaspoon baking powder	⅔ cup sugar
½ teaspoon sugar	2 teaspoons pumpkin pie
1 tablespoon sugar	spice
⅔ cup butter	2 eggs, slightly beaten
2 tablespoons cognac or	1 lb. ricotta or cottage
rum	cheese, sieved
4 tablespoons water	1½ cups mashed, cooked
	pumpkin (or canned
	pumpkin)

Pastry: sift together flour, baking powder, salt and 1 tablespoon sugar. Cut in butter until mixture is in fine, even crumbs. Add cognac and water and work into a soft dough. Turn on lightly floured surface and knead gently for half a minute. Divide dough in half. Roll half of dough out about ¼ inch thick and line a 9-inch pie plate or pan, leaving about 1 inch overhang. Roll out other half of dough about ¼ inch thick and cut into half-inch strips to form lattice top.

236

Filling: sift dry ingredients together and stir into eggs. Blend in ricotta and pumpkin and pour into prepared pie pan. Criss-cross lattice strips over top. Roll bottom crust up over ends of strips and flute deeply. Bake in a very hot 450° F. oven for 10 minutes; reduce temperature to slow 325° F. and bake 45 minutes longer, or until knife inserted in center comes out clean. Cool in oven.

RICE AND CHOCOLATE PIE, TUSCAN

PASTA FROLLA (flaky sweet pastry)

2 cups sifted flour
½ cup sugar
pinch of salt
¼ cup butter
3 eggs yolks, slightly beaten
½ teaspoon grated lemon rind
3 to 4 tablespoons milk

FILLING

1 cup rice
2¼ cups milk
⅓ cup sugar
3 squares semi-sweet chocolate, melted
1 egg, beaten
1 teaspoon finely minced citron
1 teaspoon grated lemon rind
2 tablespoons pine nuts (pignoli)
½ cup seedless raisins
½ teaspoon baking powder
1 tablespoon brandy
1 tablespoon rum
½ teaspoon vanilla

In the gay bustle of preparing Easter goodies, this pie "Torta di Pasqua" is a "must" in Tuscany households, where not one but several pies are prepared at a time. A luscious pie that keeps well indefinitely.

Prepare Pastry: sift together flour, sugar and salt. Cut in butter with pastry blender or two knives. Form a hollow in center. Place egg yolks and lemon rind in hollow, combine by hand with flour mixture and then knead until smooth. Use milk to hold mixture together. Shape into a ball; chill for 30 minutes. Divide ball into 2 parts, one larger than the other. Roll larger piece on lightly floured board into a round, ⅛ inch thick, large enough to line a 10-inch pie plate. Butter pie plate and line with bottom crust, leaving a ½-inch overhang around edge. Roll out smaller piece, ⅛ inch thick and cut into 1-inch strips.

Prepare Filling: soak raisins and nuts in warm water for about 30 minutes. Drain. Heat milk, stir in sugar, add rice and cook until rice is tender but firm and has absorbed the milk. Mixture should not be dry. Remove from heat, blend in melted chocolate and rest of ingredients. Add a little milk if mixture seems too thick or dry. Turn into prepared pie shell and spread evenly. Arrange pastry strips crisscross over filling in lattice design. Roll or fold bottom crust up over ends of strips and flute deeply. Brush pastry with beaten egg (optional) and bake in preheated 375° F. oven for 35 to 45 minutes, or until firm and golden brown.

RICOTTA CHEESE PIE

Sweet Pastry

2 cups sifted flour
1 teaspoon baking powder
½ teaspoon salt
⅔ cup butter
2 tablespoons cognac or
   rum
4 tablespoons water

Filling

1½ lbs. ricotta cheese
1 tablespoon flour

2 tablespoons chopped
   almonds
2 tablespoons toasted
   pine nuts
2 tablespoons chopped
   citron
1 teaspoon vanilla
4 eggs
1 cup sugar
confectioners' sugar

Sweet Pastry: sift dry ingredients; cut in butter with two knives or pastry blender. Add cognac gradually, and enough water until mixture will hold together. Chill. Roll out two-thirds of dough on lightly floured board into a large round, ⅛ inch thick, and line a 10-inch pie plate, leaving about ½ inch overhang. Roll remaining dough about ¼-inch thick and cut into ½-inch wide strips with pastry cutter, for lattice top.

Filling: combine first 6 ingredients; blend well. Beat eggs, adding sugar gradually while beating; add to ricotta mixture; blend until smooth. Turn into prepared pie pan. Crisscross lattice strips over top; fold edge over and flute. Bake in a preheated 400° F. oven for the first 10 minutes, lower heat to 350° F. and bake 45 minutes longer. Cool in oven. Serve sprinkled with confectioners' sugar. *Serves about 8.*

GLOSSARY

Abbachio: Roman dialect for very young spring lamb, which is a specialty of Rome.

Acciuga: anchovy.

Aglio: garlic.

Aglio e Olio: garlic and olive oil.

Agnellotti: little dough dumplings stuffed with meat and herbs, cooked in broth; a Tuscan specialty.

Al dente: a term used in cooking macaroni products—meaning "to the tooth," chewy, not cooked to a pulp.

Al forno: in the oven.

Anchovy: a small fish about 3 inches in length, packed in salt or oil, usually in fillets.

Anise: a licorice-flavored seed, used in cookies, candies and liqueurs.

Anitra: duck in general.

Antipasto: "before meal"—a term used for appetizers or hors d'oeuvres.

Baccalá: dried and salted fish, usually cod.

Basil: "basilico"—an aromatic sweet herb, species of the mint family, used in tomato sauces and dressings.

Bianco: applied to sauces without tomatoes—"white," not colored.

Bigné: a pastry puff, usually filled with a variety of creams.

Biscotti: cookies or biscuits.

Bistecca: beefsteak.

Bombette: little balls. Literal translation: tiny bombs.

240

Braciole: thin slices of meat; usually stuffed, rolled and tied.

Braised: meat cooked by first searing in fat and then allowing to simmer in a small amount of moisture.

Brioches: soft, doughy cakes or rolls, usually served as a breakfast item.

Brodetto: "little broth" in which meat or fish floats in an abundant sauce or gravy, either thick or thin.

Buongustai: gourmets.

Burgundy: a dry red wine.

Cacciatora: "hunter style," meaning food cooked in quick, simple sauces.

Cacciucco: a type of bouillabaisse, a fish soup consisting of a variety of fish and shellfish, strongly spiced.

Cannellini: white kidney beans.

Cannelloni: large tubular macaroni, usually stuffed, or squares of homemade dough stuffed and baked with a sauce.

Cannoli: pastry shells with a cream filling—a Sicilian specialty.

Capers: flower buds of the caper bush which grows in Southern Europe; pickled or packed in salt, and used for flavoring and in dressings.

Cappelletti: "little hats"; a Roman variety of the Tortellini Bolognese.

Carrozza: "in Carrozza"—"in a carriage"—a Neapolitan term applied to fried soft-cheese sandwiches.

Casalinga: "home style."

Cassata Siciliana: a rich cream cake.

Ceci: chick peas.

Chablis: a dry white wine.

Cognac: a superior quality of brandy, loosely applied to French brandies in general.

Cotoletta: a cutlet.

Costoletta: a chop.

Crostino: small squares of toasted or fried bread, usually used for canapés.

Dry: unsweetened, as applied to wines.

Escarole: the broad-leaved endive or chicory plant. The leaves are wavy instead of curled.

Fagioli: beans.

Fagiolini: green beans.

Fagottino: a "little bundle" or stuffed thin slice of meat, rolled.

Fennel: a sweet herb, the seeds of which are used for flavoring; the fragrance and taste suggests anise.

Fettuccine: homemade egg noodles, usually ⅛ to ¼ inch wide.

Fillets: term applied specifically to tenderloin of beef, to the fleshy part of a leg of veal or mutton, to the breast of a chicken, and to thick boneless slices of fish.

Fontina: a soft cheese from the northern part of Italy.

Fra Diavolo: "Brother Devil" . . . a piquant tomato sauce.

Fritto Misto: "mixed fry" of either vegetables, fish or meat.

Glacé: glazed.

Gnocchi: dumplings made either from mashed potatoes or flour.

Gorgonzola: the Italian type of French Roquefort or Danish Blue Cheese.

Gruyère: a pressed, pale yellow, whole milk cheese with a nutty flavor, made in Northern Italy and Switzerland.

Lasagne: large, broad giant noodles.

Linguine: a type of spaghetti, thin and flat, instead of round.

Luganica: an Italian sweet sausage, long and winding, not divided in links.

Maccaroncelli: a type of long-cut macaroni, resembling spaghetti but a little thick and with a small hole running through the center.

Manicotti: large tubes of fine macaroni dough, stuffed and baked in a sauce.

Marinade: a compound liquor, generally of wine, oil, vinegar, herbs and spices in which fish, meats or fowl are steeped before cooking to improve their flavor.

Marinara: "sailor style"—applied to quick tomato sauces.

Marjoram: an herb, a species of the oregano-mint family, used to flavor meats and poultry.

Marsala: an amber-colored semi-sweet wine, resembling sherry, but much heavier.

Minestrone: an Italian vegetable soup, rather thick.

Mortadella: a large type of salami, actually a bologna type of salami; originated in the city of Bologna.

Mozzarella: a soft, fresh cheese, which becomes stringy in cooking—famous as the pizza cheese.

Oregano: a distinctive strong-flavored herb used in tomato and meat sauces, pizza, stews, roasts, gravies, and dressings.

Ossobuco: "hollow-bone"—shanks, usually veal; used in a famous Milanese dish.

Panettone: "big bread," a sweet yeast bread with raisins and citron; originated in Milan.

Paprika: a sweet red pepper spice; good with shellfish, fish, creamed sauces, gravies, casseroles and dressings.

Parmigiana: applied to dishes cooked with cheese, taken from parmigiano, meaning Parmesan cheese.

Parmigiano: a hard cheese made from partly skimmed milk, with a green or black rind. Used extensively in grated form. Dishes using this cheese are referred to as "alla parmigiana."

Parmesan: Parmigiana.

Pasta: dough. Also applied to all macaroni products.

Pasticcio: timbale . . . pie: a mixture of many ingredients. A potpourri.

Pastina: a very small-cut macaroni, especially used for soups.

Perciatelli: similar to maccaroncelli but not so thick.

Pesce: fish.

Pesto: a famous Genoese green sauce used for pasta and also as a base for soups or stews; its main ingredients are garlic and basil.

Pignoli: pine nuts.

Pizza: pie or tart.

Pizzaiola: piquant tomato sauce.

Polenta: cornmeal mush.

Polpetta: meatball.

Polpettine: small meatballs.

Polpettone: meat loaf or large stuffed meat roll.

Potacchio: a style of stew (meat or fish), specialty of the Italian Adriatic coast.

Prosciutto: ham prepared in the Italian manner—dried, salted, spiced and pressed, not smoked; similar to Westphalian ham.

Provinciale: provincial, regional cooking.

Provolone: a piquant semi-hard creamy Italian cheese.

Ravioli: dough dumplings stuffed with a variety of fillings such as meats, cheeses, spinach, etc., boiled and served with sauces.

Ricotta: a cheese that resembles cottage cheese but is smoother and creamier and has a natural sweet milk flavor.

Rigatoni: ribbed tubular macaroni.

Ripieno: filling or stuffing.

Riso: rice

Risotto: cooked rice, usually cooked in chicken broth, with other condiments.

Romano: a hard, sharp white cheese, served grated like Parmesan cheese.

Rosemary: an evergreen herb resembling little pine needles. Used to flavor roasts and stews.

Saffron: rich orange-yellow powdered spice used in flavoring and coloring foods.

Sage: an herb of the mint family, used with poultry, meat and fish; in stews and roasts.

Salamí: a spiced pork product.

Salmi: stewed in wine and other ingredients, used generally in cooking game.

Saltimbocca: "jump into the mouth" . . . name given to a popular Roman dish.

Sauté: to fry quickly and lightly in hot oil or butter, while turning frequently.

Savoiardi: ladyfingers.

Scaloppine: thin slices of meat, applicable not only to veal but to other meats.

Scampi: pertaining to the shrimp family.

Semolina: the heart of the wheat, finely ground; a type of farina.

Sesame: sweet, nut-like seeds, baked on bread and rolls; used to flavor cookies, cakes and candies; and in salad dressings.

Sherry: an amber-colored semi-sweet wine.

Soffritto: a fried spicy base for soups, sauces or meat dishes.

Stecchini: small skewers or toothpicks.

Spumone: an Italian frozen cream, a type of ice cream.

Stracciatella: an egg-drop soup.

Suffli: Italian for "soufflé." A light and frothy dish, usually baked.

Thyme: distinctive, pleasantly flavored herb, used in fish, chowders, tomatoes, salads and poultry stuffing.

Tufoli: giant tubular macaroni which are stuffed.

Vermicelli: very fine spaghetti.

Vongole: clams. The Italian variety is much smaller than the American littleneck.

Zabaione or Zabaglione: a wine-egg cream or custard dessert, served warm or cold in glasses.

Ziti: a large-cut macaroni of the tubular type.

Zucchini: Italian squash; a form of summer squash, dark green, cylindrical and slightly curved, with thick tender flesh and a thin skin which is never peeled off.

Zuppa Inglese: "English soup," a dessert made of ladyfingers or sponge cake, rum and a pastry cream. Similar to English "trifle."

INDEX

APPETIZERS:
Chicken Liver & Anchovy
Canapé, 4
Clams, Baked Oregano, 3
Cocktail Coral Sauce for Sea-
food, *see Sauces,* 184
Meatballs, Florentine, *see
Beef,* 65
Shrimp, Broiled, Gourmet, 4
Shrimp, Oven Fried Curried in
Dip, 5

BEEF:
Beef Slices, Pizzaiola, 59
Boiled, Casserole with Vege-
tables, 60
Egg Stuffed Roll, Sicilian, 61
Fillet in Marsala & Cognac, 62
Fillet, Roast, Marinated, 64
Fillets, Neapolitan, 63
Goulash, Hungarian, 65
Meat Pie, Oriental, 66
Meatballs, Florentine, 65
Omelet Stuffed Roll, 67
Pot Roast in Burgundy, 68
Sauerbraten, 69
Steak Surprises, 70
Stew in Red Wine, 72
Stew with Fennel, 71
Stuffed Roll, Sicilian, 74

Stuffed Rolls, Neapolitan (Bra-
ciole), 73
Surprise Roast Roll, 75
Tenderloin in Pastry, 76
Tripe alla Fiorentina, 77
Tripe alla Romana, 78

CAKES:
Apple Torte Layer Cake, 209
Baba Rum, 209
Cheese, My Favorite, 210
Cheese, with Raisins, 211
Mocha Chiffon, 212
Cream (Cassata), 213
Orange Rum Ring, 213
Panettone, Sweet Raisin Bread,
Milanese, 214
Peach, French, 215
Rum, Italian, 216
Savarin, Fruit, 217
Savoy Ring Cake, 218
Spice, Italian, 218

COOKIES:
Anise Biscuits, 219
Florentine, 219
Macaroons, Italian, 220
Pine Nut Cookies, 220
Sesame, Queen's Biscuits, 221

DESSERTS:
Crepes, Italian, Flambé, 222
Rice Fritters, Florentine, 223
Spumone, 223
Strawberry Fritters, 224
Zabaione or Zabaglione, 225
Zuppa Inglese, 225

EGGS (and CHEESE):
Baked in Tomato Cases, 17
Baked with Potatoes & Cheese, 17
Egg and Cheese Pie, 18
Eggs in Tomato Sauce, 18
Eggs, Parmesan Style, 18
Fried, Cheese Stuffed, 19
Manicotti "Quick," 19
Omelette, Mozzarella, Baked, 20

FISH:
Bass, Baked with Potatoes & Tomato Sauce, 25
Carp, Stuffed Baked in White Wine, 26
Clam, Baked, Oregano, see Appetizers, 3
Clam Soup, Neapolitan, 27
Cod, Salted, Roman Style, 27
Flounder, Fillet, Piquant, 28
Frogs' Legs in Fresh Tomato Sauce, 29
Fry, Mixed, Marinated, 29
Lobster all'Americana, 30
Lobster fra Diavolo, 31
Shrimp, broiled, Gourmet, see Appetizers, 4
Shrimp in Tomato and White Wine Sauce, 32
Shrimp, Marinara, 32
Squid in Tomato Sauce, 34
Squid, Stuffed, 33
Stew, Tuscan Style (Cacciucco), 35
Trout, Stuffed Baked, 35
Whiting, Baked with Mushrooms & Wine, 36
Whiting, Savory Steamed, 37

ITALIAN SPECIALTIES:
Cornmeal Mush (Polenta), 201

ITALIAN SPECIALTIES (cont.)
Gnocchi, Potato, 202
Gnocchi, Ricotta, 201
Mozzarella, Sandwich, Fried (in Carrozza), 205
Pizza Capricious, see Pizza, Neapolitan, 203
Pizza, Neapolitan, 203
Polenta, 201

LAMB:
Braised, Easter Style, 79
Cacciatora, Roman Style, 80
Chops in Pastry, 81
Chops in Wine, 82
Diced with Peas & White Wine, 83
Leg, Sauerbraten, 83
Leg, Stuffed, Renaissance, 84
Shoulder, Roast, Renaissance, 85
Shoulder, Stuffed, 86
Stew, with Artichokes, 87
Stew, with olives, Country Style (Pottachio), 87

LASAGNE:
with Tomatoless Meat & Dry Mushroom Sauce, 155
with Meat Sauce, 153
with Spinach, Chicken Liver Sauce, 154

MACARONI:
Baked in Two Sauces, 157
Baked, with Eggplant, 156
Cannelloni, Sicilian, 158
Casserole, Sausage, Egg Topping, 159
in Piquant Sauce, 162
Manicotti, 161
Manicotti, Quick, see Eggs, "Crepes," 19
Pot-Pourri with Chicken Livers, 162
Ravioli, Meat, see Ravioli with Ricotta, 164
Ravioli, Neapolitan, 163
Ravioli with Ricotta, 164
Timbale with Mushrooms, 167
with Seafood Sauce, 165

NOODLES:
  Dumplings, Stuffed, Bologna Style, 168
  Dumplings, Stuffed, Tuscan, 170
  Egg Noodles, Home Made, 172
  Egg Noodles with butter, cream and cheese (Fettuccine all' Alfredo), 171
  Fettuccine all'Alfredo, *see Egg noodles with butter, cream and cheese*, 171
  Green Egg Noodles, 174
  with Garlic & Basil Sauce, Genovese (Pesto), 173

PASTRY:
  Brioche, 226
  Cannoli alla Siciliana, 227
  Cream Puffs, 229
  Easter Cream Puff Dessert, 230
  Honey Balls or Bubbles, 231
  Pasticiotti, Neapolitan, 232
  Ribbons & Bows, 233
  Tartlets (Cassatine), 234

PIES:
  Fruit Roll, 235
  Pumpkin Cheese, 236
  Rice and Chocolate, Tuscan, 237
  Ricotta Cheese, 239

PORK:
  Braised, Piquant Sauce, 89
  Chops, Neapolitan, 90
  Chops with Herbs, 90
  Ham, Roast Fresh, Stuffed, 91
  Loin of Pork in Red Wine, 92
  Loin, Roast, Adriatic, 92
  Sausages and Mushrooms with Polenta, 93
  Sausages and Peppers, 94
  Stew, Savory, 94

POTATOES:
  Baked, Stuffed, 137
  Croquettes, 138
  Pie, Stuffed, Gourmet, 139
  Potato Brioches, 138
  Potato Pizza (Pie), 139

POULTRY:
  Capon, Stuffed, Gourmet, 41
  Chicken, Baked in Savory Crumbs, 42
  Chicken, Batter Baked, Piedmont, 42
  Chicken Breasts, Cheese Baked with Broccoli, 43
  Chicken Breasts, Rice and Mushrooms, 44
  Chicken Cacciatora, Hunter Style, 45
  Chicken Flambé, 45
  Chicken, Hunter Style, with Olives, 46
  Chicken Livers with Sage, 47
  Chicken, Marinated, Fried, Florentine, 47
  Chicken, Roast, Stuffed with Beef and Spinach, 49
  Chicken Stew, Rosemary, 50
  Chicken with Prosciutto and Mushrooms, 48
  Duck in Salmi, 53
  Duck, Palermo Style, 51
  Duck, Paté Stuffed, 52
  Squabs in Foil, 54
  Turkey, Roast, Stuffed, Lombardy, 55,

RICE:
  Balls, Cheese Stuffed, 143
  Croquettes, Meat Stuffed, 143
  Risotto, Milanese, 147
  with Cauliflower, 144
  with Eggplant, Parmesan, 145
  with Fresh Tomato Sauce, 146
  with Mushrooms, Fedora, 146
  with Shrimp Sauce, Adriatic, 148

SALADS:
  Artichoke, Stuffed, Salad, 193
  Bean and Tuna Salad, Italian, 193
  Caesar, 194
  Cauliflower, Neapolitan Style, 195
  Green Bean & Stuffed Tomato, 196
  Green Bean, Savory, 195

SALADS (*cont.*)
  Potato, Continental, 196
  Zucchini, 197

SAUCES:
  Beef, Braised, Tomatoless, 183
  Clam, Red, *see Spaghetti,* 178
  Clam, White, see *Spaghetti,* 180
  Coral, Cocktail, for Seafood, 184
  Meat Ball, *see Spaghetti,* 176
  Meat, Chopped, with Tomatoes,
    Neapolitan, 184
  Meat, Mushrooms, Tomatoes and
    Sausages, 185
  Pesto, *see Egg Noodles with
    Garlic & Basil Sauce, Geno-
    vese,* 173
  Pot Roast, with Mushrooms, for
    Macaroni, 186
  Ragout, Bologna Style, 187
  Ragout of Sausages & Mush-
    rooms, 188
  Tomato, Neapolitan, 184
  Tomato, "Quick," 189
  Tuna Sauce for Spaghetti, 189
  Vinaigrette, Green, with An-
    chovies, 190

SOUPS:
  Bean and Macaroni, alla Ro-
    mana, 9
  Chicken Vegetable, with Meat-
    balls, 10
  Egg-Drop, Roman, 10
  Onion and Egg, 11
  Vegetable and Bean, Florentine,
    12

SPAGHETTI:
  alla Marinara, 175
  Vermicelli Casserole with Meats
    & Vegetables, 179
  with Eggplant, Sicilian, 175
  with Meat Balls, 176
  with Oil, Garlic & Anchovy
    Sauce, 177
  with Red Clam Sauce, 178
  with White Clam Sauce, 180

VEAL:
  and Peppers, Neapolitan, 104
  Birds, Cacciatora (Hunter Style),
    96
  Birds, Chicken Livers, en Bro-
    chette, 97
  Birds, Tomato Sauce, 98
  Braised with Carrots, 98
  Breast, Stuffed, 99
  Chops in Casserole, 100
  Chops, "Othello," 101
  Cutlet, Parmesan, 102
  Fricassee with Mushrooms, 102
  Kidneys, Trifolati, 103
  in Tuna Sauce, 105
  Rolls, Stuffed, al Marsala, 106
  Saltimbocca alla Romana, 106
  Scaloppine al Marsala, 108
  Scaloppine, Fancy, 107
  Scaloppine, Prosciutto and
    Wine, 109
  Shanks, Milanese (Ossobuco),
    110
  Stew with Marjoram and Toma-
    toes, 111

VEGETABLES:
  Artichokes alla Romana, 116
  Artichokes, Jewish Style, 115
  Artichokes, Sausage Stuffed, 117
  Artichokes, Stuffed, Sicilian, 118
  Asparagus with Prosciutto au
    Gratin, 119
  Broccoli, Sicilian Style, 119
  Eggplant Parmesan, 120
  Eggplant Sandwiches, 121
  Eggplant Timbale, 121
  Eggplant with Olives in Tomato
    Sauce, 120
  Green Beans in Tomato Sauce,
    122
  Lentils, Home Style, 123
  Lettuce, Stuffed Leaves, 123
  Mushrooms in Tomato Sauce,
    125
  Mushrooms, Ricotta Stuffed, 124
  Onions, Artichoke & Shrimp
    Stuffed, 125
  Peas, Roman Style, 126

VEGETABLES (*cont.*)
  Peppers in Piquant Sauce, 126
  Peppers, Stuffed, Neapolitan,
    127
  Peppers, Upside Down, Stuffed,
    128
  Spinach in Tomato Sauce, 129
  Spinach, Olive Oil & Garlic, 128

VEGETABLES (*cont.*)
  Tomatoes, Eggplant Stuffed, 129
  Vegetable Fry, Mix, 130
  Zucchini, Fried, Julienne, 131
  Zucchini in Tomato Sauce, 132
  Zucchini, Mozzarella, Pan-
    cooked, 132
  Zucchini, Tuna Fish Stuffed, 133